Steaming Through Three Counties

Steaming Through Three Counties

A personal record of journeys
and visits 1955-1966

Gerald Adams

SLP

Silver Link Publishing Ltd

First published in 2010

British Library Cataloguing in Publication Data

A catalogue record for this book is available from the British Library.

ISBN 978 1 85794 350 4

Silver Link Publishing Ltd
The Trundle
Ringstead Road
Great Addington
Kettering
Northants NN14 4BW

Tel/Fax: 01536 330588
email: sales@nostalgiacollection.com
Website: www.nostalgiacollection.com

Printed and bound in the Czech Republic

Prints of the photographs in this book are available from John Stretton (j.stret@zen.co.uk)

The publisher is grateful to Zoe White for transcribing the original manuscript.

Half title **22 March 1958: 'Modified Hall' Class 4-6-0 No 6992** *Arborfield Hall* **climbs the bank through Rowley Regis & Blackheath station with the 7.20am Hereford to Birmingham (Snow Hill) train. I took this photograph through the front window of the 8.48am diesel multiple unit from Birmingham (Snow Hill) to Bewdley as it approached the station.**

Title page **6 April 1963: The Chalford auto-trains called at all the halts on the Great Western line from Gloucester to Swindon, terminating at Chalford at the head of the Stroud Valley. Here we see ex-GWR 0-4-2T No 1472 calling at Downfield Crossing Halt with a train for Gloucester. The fireman is probably looking out for a signal from the driver in the driving compartment at the head of the train before starting; the regulator operation from the auto-carriage did not always function very well, so the fireman drove the train from the footplate of the locomotive and the driver joint-controlled the braking.**

Below **27 September 1956: ex-GWR 'Hall' Class 4-6-0 No 4988** *Bulwell Hall* **on a Worcester to Birmingham train climbs Old Hill bank approaching Rowley Regis & Blackheath. The milepost behind the locomotive is the distance from Paddington via Oxford and Worcester, the Oxford, Worcester & Wolverhampton Railway route, known locally as the 'Old Worse and Worse'.**

Contents

Above **26 April 1958:** During the late 1950s the Stephenson Locomotive Society (Midland Area) ran many special trains, and the author took part in a large number of them. This is the SLS special that formed the last train on the Bromyard to Leominster line, which had been closed and out of use since September 1952. Participants on the special had a 10-minute stop to explore the undergrowth round Fencote station.

Opposite page **: 29 August 1964:** Ex-GWR 'Castle' Class 4-6-0 No 5056 *Earl of Powis* is ready to leave Cheltenham Spa (Malvern Road) station on a summer Saturday train taking the author back to Birmingham (Snow Hill) after a visit to Gloucester (see also page 120). The clear signal indicates the line to Stratford-upon-Avon; the other is for the short branch line into Cheltenham Spa (St James) station. Both stations were closed on 3 January 1966.

Preface

*O*ur Dad was a keen railway enthusiast for all his life. His particular passion was steam. As a boy he would spend hours watching trains in the Birmingham area, then as an adult he had the opportunity to travel all over the world, and he travelled by rail wherever possible.

His love of trains saw him go on holiday to Hong Kong, but rather than fly he travelled there by rail from Ledbury station, in Herefordshire. He was very proud to have travelled by train in all but two US states (North and South Dakota). Dad kept meticulous records of his travels, from engine details to mapping all the lines in the UK he travelled on. He built up an extensive photographic library and regularly spoke to groups about his travels.

This book was written about three of the counties in which he had travelled extensively. Unfortunately he never got to see the book published as, while on a rail holiday in Alaska in 2000, he suffered a fatal coronary aneurism.

As a family we are extremely proud to see this book published, and hope that you enjoy seeing his photos of a bygone era of rail travel.

Paul Adams, Suzanne Adams, Jenny Court,

Rachel Taylor and Clare Adams

Introduction

This book has been produced as a result of well-meaning friends, who have seen my personal collection of photographs, suggesting that I should do so.

My photograph collection was only ever intended as a personal record of journeys and visits made. The majority were taken between 1955 and 1965, and cover many parts of England and Wales.

In order to make the book interesting a theme was considered essential to give meaning to the collection; a random assortment from all over the place with huge areas not included would be unsatisfactory.

When the photographs were taken I lived first in Birmingham, then Gloucester, and most of my journeys were on British Railways (Western Region). After months of sorting and examining, I thought that my photographs in Gloucestershire, Herefordshire and Worcestershire could be made into a book, and these 'Cathedral Counties' could be the theme. However, after collating all the photographs strictly in this category and discarding those of very poor quality, there were insufficient to produce an acceptable book. The next thought was to borrow pictures from other photographers to fill the book, but this would defeat the objective of producing 'my' book, so it became necessary to expand the area covered. The outcome of this was that I invented a set of rules: all the photographs must have been taken within or not more than 10 miles outside the historical boundaries of the three counties (all of which have fine Cathedrals), and any taken outside the boundaries but within the 10-mile rule must have a connection with the counties. It will be obvious that these rules now meant that relevant photographs in the whole of the Birmingham and Bristol areas together with Swindon could be included.

Having made the rules I had then to set about producing the best quality prints I could. Fortunately I had kept my negatives properly filed in tissue paper negative files of pre-war vintage, they were indexed and a register had been kept over the years. The register is my only record of the dates of the photographs and sketchy details of the locations, and I am sure that there are errors.

A large amount of searching through old journal notes, old trainspotting notes and old timetables resulted in the descriptions given to the photographs. I have also referred to friends for further information and correction and I must thank them for so cheerfully giving me information and advice. During the preparation of the captions I also referred to the following books and papers: Pathfinder Railtours tour booklets; Stephenson Locomotive Society (Midland Area) itineraries and notes; and *Steam Around Gloucester* by Norman Preedy (Peter Watts Publishing).

Gerald Adams

1955

Above **14 March 1955:** My first photograph with my own camera was of ex-Midland Railway 0-6-0 No 43594 taking the line through Kings Norton station towards Birmingham (New Street), so I assume it would have terminated at one of the goods yards before reaching New Street. Any earlier photographs were taken with my father's camera.

Below **14 March 1955:** The second photograph taken at Kings Norton station on the same day shows LMS 'Crab' 2-6-0 No 42846 on a freight from the Camp Hill line heading westward through the platform, which was disused at that time but provided access to the footbridge (from which the photograph was taken) that led to the active platforms on the line to Birmingham New Street via Selly Oak.

Below **21 March 1955: Known locally as the 'Dudley Dodger', ex-GWR 0-4-2T No 1414 in 'pull' mode enters Birmingham (Snow Hill) station with a service from Dudley. Note the ancient push-pull carriage. This service was operated by '1400' Class 0-4-2T engines and some ancient coaches, or the ex-GWR diesel railcars.**

Below **11 April 1955: An express from the West of England to the North hauled by GWR 'Castle' Class 4-6-0 No 5028** *Llantilio Castle* **races through Craven Arms.**

Above 30 April 1955: During early 1955 it was necessary to withdraw from use the whole of the GWR 'King' Class in order to strengthen the front ends of the main frames; this caused a motive power shortage on the Western Region resulting in the borrowing of some powerful locomotives from the Midland Region. Former LMS 4-6-2 'Coronation' Class No 46237 *City of Bristol* heads a Wolverhampton to Paddington train through Widney Manor station.

Below 21 May 1955: The Stephenson Locomotive Society (Midland Area) organised a special train to the Cleobury Mortimer & Ditton Priors Light Railway hauled by former GWR 'Dean Goods' 0-6-0 No 2516. It is seen here at Kidderminster station. (*Above left* Platform poster detail - Billy Graham at Wembley and promoting the delights of Somerset)

6 August 1955: In this busy scene at Birmingham (Snow Hill) station, 'Hall' Class 4-6-0 4998 *Eyton Hall* has arrived from the Southern Region, while 2-6-0 No 9319 waits on the centre track for a train ahead to enter the tunnel, and 2-6-2T No 4172 waits to proceed to Tyseley shed after arrival from Stourbridge Junction.

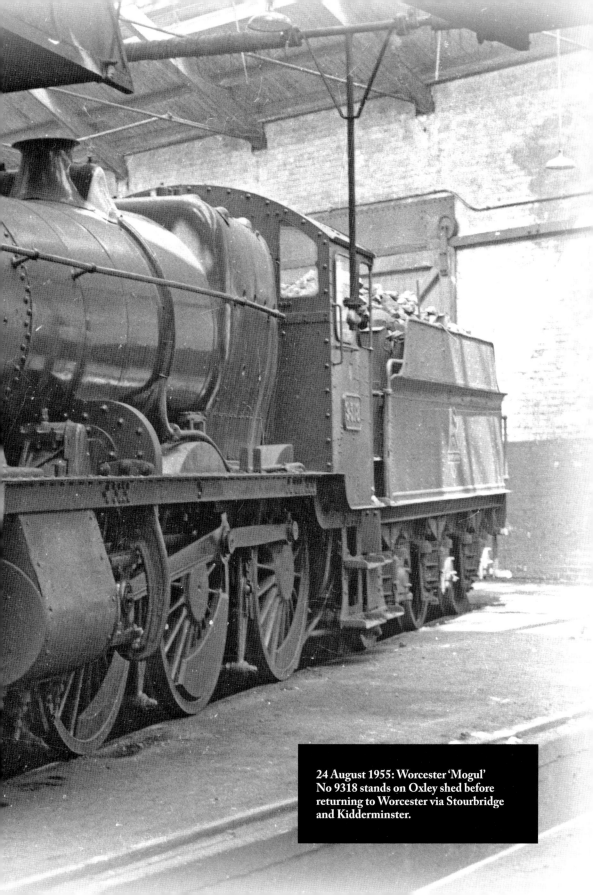

24 August 1955: Worcester 'Mogul' No 9318 stands on Oxley shed before returning to Worcester via Stourbridge and Kidderminster.

SLS Star special, 11 September 1955			
Station	Arrive	Depart	Loco(s)
Birmingham (Snow Hill)		9.28am	4061
Tyseley		9.35	
Stratford-Upon-Avon		10.11	
Swindon Works, Rodbourne Lane Siding	1.15pm	4.40	
Didcot	5.18	5.55	
Oxford via Honeybourne East	6.12	7.17	
Stratford-upon-Avon	8.16		
Lapworth	8.52		
Tyseley	9.07		
Birmingham (Snow Hill)	9.14		

Top left **11 September 1955:** The loco crew of ex-GWR 'Star' Class 4-6-0 No 4061 *Glastonbury Abbey* pose in front of the locomotive at the Rodbourne Lane siding at Swindon Works after bringing in the Stephenson Locomotive Society Star Special from Birmingham (Snow Hill) via Stratford-upon-Avon and Bristol into Swindon 20 minutes early. Participants in the tour detrained in the siding by either climbing down or using steps provided to some doors. The train returned to Snow Hill via Didcot, Oxford and Honeybourne east curve.

Bottom left **11 September 1955:** 'Castle' Class 4-6-0 No 5050 *Earl of St Germans*, in sparkling ex-works condition, took over a North East of England to South Wales train at Swindon, proceeding via the Badminton line and the Severn Tunnel. Note the LNER teak coach next to the engine.

Below **27 December 1955:** The locomotive hired for the film *The Titfield Thunderbolt*, GWR 0-4-2T No 1401, was photographed at Honeybourne propelling a very ancient auto-coach. The photograph was taken while on a post-Christmas cycle ride, and I have no record of the time or train.

Below **27 December 1955:** The Ashchurch-Evesham-Alcester-Redditch-Birmingham line was normally worked by 2-6-0 tender engines or 2-6-4Ts. This view of a Redditch-bound train was taken as it passed the disused station at Wixford hauled by Fowler 2-6-4T No 42337. The station had closed in 1950 and the line closed in 1962. The carriage set of this train is a complete set of Midland Railway compartment stock with Brake Compartments at both outer ends.

1956

Above **14 February 1956: A snowy St Valentine's Day at Kings Heath station welcomes ex-LMS 0-6-0s Nos 43976 and** *(below)* **43863, both on their way from the west towards the Saltley area. The station had closed to passengers on 27 November 1946.**

Above **14 March 1956: LMS 'Jubilee' 4-6-0 No 45555** *Quebec* **pulls put of Smethwick station with a train for Wolverhampton. Note the remnants of an old gas lamp in the foreground.**

Below **18 March 1956: Bristol (Barrow Road) shed was coded 22A in 1956, when this photograph of ex-LMS 0-6-0T No 47552 and ex-Midland 2F 0-6-0T No 41706 was taken. This part of Bristol was in Gloucestershire at that time. The rail-mounted ash wagons both at rail level and in the pit between the tracks are unusual features of this shed yard.**

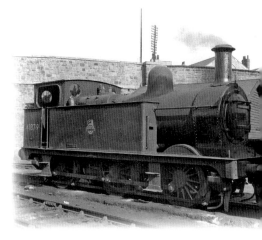

Above **18 March 1956: Also on Barrow Road shed that day was ex-Midland 0-6-0T No 41879.**

Left **23 March 1956: Galton Junction, Smethwick, was where the former GWR line into Birmingham (Snow Hill) crossed the LNWR line from Birmingham (New Street) to Wolverhampton (High Level). Ex-LNWR 0-8-0 No 49313 is hauling a breakdown train towards Wolverhampton.**

Top right **23 March 1956: Today's new Smethwick Galton Bridge station is situated exactly where this Liverpool to Birmingham train is seen. Ex-LMS 'Patriot' Class 4-6-0 No 45505** *The Royal Army Ordnance Corps* **was not rebuilt with a taper boiler and continued with a narrow Midland-type tender up to its withdrawal. Although this Black Country location appears to have little connection with the 'Cathedral Counties', both lines are in Worcestershire only a short distance north and west of this point when they enter Oldbury.**

Bottom right **2 April 1956: Lydney Junction was a sub-shed to Gloucester, and 0-6-0PT No 1631 is parked there with its bunker amply filled with a mixture of coal and cobbles. This type of light pannier tank was the most numerous at that time, being ideally suited to work the remaining lines in the Forest of Dean. On the day of this photograph the shed and yard contained Nos 1623/5/7/30/1, 7741, 1430 and 2248.**

Above **23 June 1956 and 16 April 1990:
The same locomotive in the same
place 34 years apart. In the older view
'Castle' Class 4-6-0 No 5080** *Defiant*,
**on the 3.45pm Birmingham to Swansea
train, passes through Shirley. In 1990
(***Left***) the same locomotive is on 'The
Shakespeare Express', the 12.50 Tyseley
to Stratford-upon-Avon special. The
major changes over the years are the loss
of the footbridge roof and parcels trolley
crossing, and the change of signal from
lower to upper quadrant.**

Below **19 August 1956: In this general
view inside the double roundhouse at
Oxley shed the locomotives present
include a Robinson 2-8-0 of the 'ROD'
Class, 3000 series, situated to the
right of the through road and with its
smokebox open.**

SLS Swindon Works special, 9 September 1956			
Station	Arrive	Depart	Loco(s)
Birmingham (Snow Hill)		9.43	4056
Hereford (Barton)	11.48	12.25pm	
Severn Tunnel Junction	2.00	2.50	
Swindon Works Siding	4.03	6.25	
Stratford-upon-Avon	8.27		
Birmingham (Snow Hill)	9.10		

Below **9 September 1956:** Ex-GWR 4-6-0 No 4056 *Princess Margaret*, **hauling the Stephenson Locomotive Society special from Birmingham Snow Hill to Swindon Works via Hereford and Severn Tunnel Junction, is standing adjacent to Hereford shed on the Hereford Barton line, which avoided the station.**

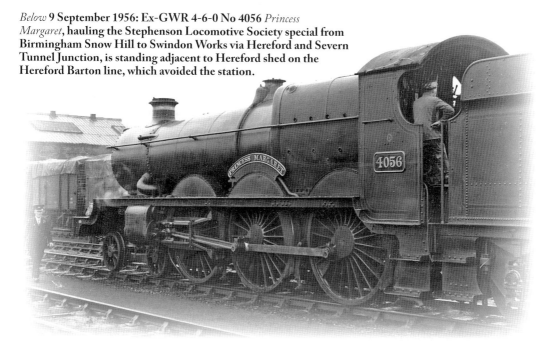

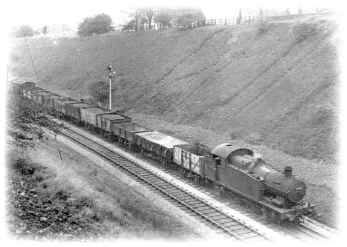

Left **27 September 1956: The top part of Old Hill Bank at Rowley Regis & Blackheath is in a deep cutting with a footpath along the top, which gave this opportunity for an unusual picture of ex-GWR 0-6-2T No 5658 with a mixed freight.**

18 November 1956: Stored out of use at Worcester, 4-4-0 'Dukedog' No 9025 stands in the sidings of the locomotive repair shop adjacent to Worcester (Shrub Hill) station minus its tender and with a sheet tied over its chimney.

Interlude: The Lickey Incline, 1954-60

Between Bromsgrove and Blackwell, the Lickey Incline was the steepest main-line gradient in Britain, and was only 11 miles from my home until I moved in 1961. Many trips to the lineside were made from 1955 onwards, mainly to Vigo, where there was an occupation level crossing about half a mile from the summit.

Above **26 February 1954: The first photograph I took on the incline, using a borrowed 116 Sye bellows camera, was of two 'Jinty' 0-6-0Ts, Nos 47313 and 47305, banking a freight train.**

Right **21 April 1954: Three bankers were required to help 'The Devonian' hauled by No 45699** *Galatea* **– 3F 0-6-0 No 43462 and 'Jinty' 0-6-0Ts Nos 47638 and 47276.**

Right **21 April 1954: After banking duties the bankers descended the incline under permissive block rules, meaning that light engines could follow one another down in procession with no signals between them. This is happening here as 'Big Bertha', the special Lickey 'Decapod' 0-10-0 banker, No 58100, follows the trio seen in the previous photo.**

Below **16th April 1955: 'Big Bertha' brings up the rear with a vengeance. No 58100 had blanketed the area with its smoke for 36 years before this photograph was taken of it banking a freight with a GWR 'Toad' brake-van.**

Above **16 April 1955: A rare sight on the Lickey – Western 'Castle' Class 4-6-0 No 7017** *G. J. Churchward* **storms up the incline with 'The Lickey Limited' (Paddington-Bristol-Birmingham New Street-Paddington) excursion organised by Ian Allan, publisher of** *Trains Illustrated*. **The 'Castle' was taken off at Kings Norton, and the train then proceeded through New Street and St Andrew's Junction to Bordesley Junction, from where another 'Castle', No 7007** *Great Western*, **returned the train to Paddington.**

Below **16 April 1955: The rear of the excursion was graced by the 'beaver-tail' Observation Car built for the pre-Second World War 'Coronation' express of the LNER. The Lickey banker 'Big Bertha' was used to bank the train, producing this unique scene. It was discovered after the event that this coach should not have been banked, but after what must have been the heaviest banking possible on British Railways no harm was done to it.**

Opposite top: **16 April 1955: An express from Bristol to the North of England climbs the incline with steam to spare. LMS 'Jubilee' 4-6-0 No 45597** *Barbados* **appears to be leaving the heavy work to its bankers.**

Opposite centre & bottom of page: **26 December 1955: Boxing Day was quite busy on the Lickey bank – LMS Class 5 4-6-0 No 44920 is hauling an express banked by 0-10-0 No 58100 and 'Jinty' 0-6-0T No 47308.**

Below: **13 April 1957: By 1957 most of the 'Jinty' 0-6-0Ts had been replaced by Western 0-6-0PTs of the '9400' Class. In this view Nos 8404 and 8401 are banking an express.**

13 April 1957: A period study of steam and telegraph poles, now both long absent from the Lickey scene. 4F 0-6-0 No 43949 from Saltley shed pounds away, with rear-end banking assistance from a single 'Jinty', *(above)* No 47638. The latter's work appears to be over as the driver nonchalantly watches the photographer.

Left **8 May 1958: In 1958 trial use was made of a GWR heavy goods 2-8-0T as a banker. No 5226 is being used here in conjunction with 0-6-0PT No 8400 to bank an express up the incline.**

Centre **8th May 1958: 2-8-0T No 5226 is seen again very near the top of the incline at Blackwell, banking an express.**

Below **8 May 1958: Standing in Blackwell station about to descend the incline, ex-MR 2P 4-4-0 No 40501 is on a local train to Worcester. Passengers wanting to board trains down the incline to Bromsgrove were required to cross the line by the boardwalk under the front of the locomotive. The footpath alongside the track on the down side was used by shunters to pin down the brakes of descending freight trains.**

Below top 8 May 1958: Each afternoon in 1958 a Worcester to Birmingham (New Street) stopping passenger train conveyed a tank wagon at the rear. MR 2P 4-4-0 No 40489 is being banked by 0-6-0PT No 8400.

Centre 8 May 1958: An optical illusion – this is not a train being banked *down* the incline, but tender-first ex-MR 3F No 43762 hauling a freight up, and being banked by 0-6-0PT No 8405.

Bottom 8 August 1959: 'Jubilee' 4-6-0 No 45682 *Trafalgar* is on 'The Devonian', the Paignton to Bradford express, on this summer Saturday, banked by 0-6-0PT No 8404 and BR 2-10-0 No 92231.

Above 8 August 1959: Another summer Saturday train, from the West of England to Sheffield, composed of a varied collection of coaches of LMS, LNER and BR origin, is hauled up the incline at 3.30pm by Stanier Class 5 No 44853. The local trainspotters have roamed from the crossing, but no one seems to mind!

Below 8 August 1959: The two 0-6-0PT bankers, Nos 8404 and 8401, seem to be doing most of the work as BR 2-10-0 No 92164 and its train climb the bank with a train to Leicester from the West of England.

Above 6 June 1960: Caprotti valve-gear LMS Class 5 No 44753 tackles the bank with an unidentified train.

Left 6 June 1960: The Lickey banker on that day was BR 2-10-0 No 92079, which was fitted with the headlight that had been worn by the 0-10-0 banker, No 58100. Here it is seen banking the train in the previous photograph.

Right 6 June 1960: BR 2-10-0 No 92079 is seen again banking a train up the incline while an LMS 0-6-0 descends with a three-coach local train.

1957

Above **22 April 1957: The Caprotti valve-gear of BR 5MT No 73132 shows clearly in this photograph of the locomotive heading north out of Craven Arms with a Hereford to Shrewsbury train.**

Below **30 April 1957: The 5.45pm train from Birmingham (Snow Hill) to Worcester (Shrub Hill) via Stratford-upon-Avon and Evesham arrives at Shirley at 5.59pm behind ex-GWR 'Hall' Class 4-6-0 No 4988** *Bulwell Hall.*

Above 8 June 1957: Spring Road is the first station on the North Warwickshire line from Tyseley to Stratford-upon-Avon, which passes through Worcestershire for a short distance near Wythall. In this photograph ex-GWR 'Manor' Class 4-6-0 No **7821** *Ditcheat Manor* is hauling a freight for Stoke Gifford yard near Bristol (where Bristol Parkway station is now situated). The fixed Distant signal at the end of the nearside platform is for Tyseley South.

Right 8 June 1957: No 3101, one of the five '3100' Class 2-6-2Ts that were rebuilds of earlier '3150' Class 2-6-2Ts with higher boiler pressure and smaller wheels, stands at Hall Green station with a train for Birmingham (Moor Street) from Henley-in-Arden.

8 June 1957: A tranquil Great Western scene as 2-6-2T No 4127 stands at Shirley station with a local train to Henley-in-Arden.

Below top **16 June 1957: What a collection of chimneys on display in front of 'Castle' Class 4-6-0 No 5000** *Launceston Castle* **at Swindon Works! This locomotive was shedded at Swindon and often worked the Paddington to Cheltenham express.**

Bottom **16 June 1957: Gloucester (Horton Road)-based ex-GWR 2-6-0 No 4358 has been beautifully turned out by Swindon Works in fully lined green and is seen here standing in Swindon shed yard prior to its return to Gloucester.**

SLS Usk-Monmouth Centenary tour, 12 October 1957			
Station	Arrive	Depart	Loco(s)
Pontypool Road		12.45pm	4668
Usk	1.05	1.10	
Llandenny	1.31	1.44	
Monmouth Troy	2.55	3.10	
Usk	4.45	4.50	
Pontypool Road	5.10		

Above **12 October 1957: GWR 0-6-0PT No 4668 was the locomotive for the special Usk-Monmouth Centenary tour, seen here at Monmouth (Troy), although the line had been closed and derelict since 28 May 1955 and was specially opened for the return passage of this train. The building behind the locomotive was a refreshment room and bar, which remained open for many years after the lines finally closed in 1959.**

Above **12 October 1957: Monmouth (Troy) station is seen from the road over the top of the tunnel mouth on the line to Usk and Pontypool Road. In the background can be seen the two bridges over the River Wye; the line to the left went to Ross-on-Wye and that to the right to Chepstow, and the coaches in the right-hand platform were used on the remaining services to both places.**

1958

22 March 1958, using service trains			
Station	Arrive	Depart	Loco(s)
Shirley		8.29am	DMU
Birmingham Snow Hill	8.45	8.48	DMU
Bewdley	10.00	11.10	W20W
Woofferton	11.58	12.10pm	6932
Shrewsbury	1.25	1.45	82007
Bridgnorth	2.44	3.04	82007
Bewdley	3.40	4.42	W22W
Hartlebury	4.56	5.17	6974
Worcester (Shrub Hill)	5.41	5.45	9486
Stratford-upon-Avon	6.51	7.17	DMU
Shirley	8.00		

Below **22 March 1958:** Tenbury Wells was the penultimate stop for the 11.10am train from Bewdley to Woofferton, consisting of former Great Western diesel railcar No W20W. The service on the Wyre Forest line was operated by these railcars for many years up its cessation in 1962.

Above **22 March 1958: Waiting to leave Bridgnorth with the 3.04pm to Bewdley, BR Standard 2-6-2T No 82007 is taking water. This station is now the northern terminus of the Severn Valley Railway and rarely sees a train of only three coaches, and never an '82000' 2-6-2T, as none survived into preservation.**

Below **22 March 1958: Hartlebury was the junction station for the lines from Worcester to Kidderminster and to Stourport-on-Severn and Bewdley, the 'Severn Valley line'. Ex-GWR 0-6-0PT No 3607 hauls a mixed freight towards Worcester at 5.00pm.**

Last train on the Bromyard to Leominster branch, 26 April 1958			
Station	Arrive	Depart	Loco(s)
Worcester (Shrub Hill)		3.10pm	4571
Worcester (Foregate Street)	3.13	3.15	
Bromyard	3.48	3.55	
Rowden Mill	4.05	4.15	
Fencote	4.25	4.35	
Steens Bridge	4.49	4.59	
Leominster	5.13	5.30	
Bromyard	6.05	6.30	
Worcester (Foregate Street)	7.03	7.05	
Worcester (Shrub Hill)	7.08		

Below **26 April 1958: One of the most unusual special trains ever organised by the Stephenson Locomotive Society (Midland Area) by the late W. A. Camwell was the last train on the Bromyard to Leominster line. The line had been closed and out of use since September 1952, but 'the track had remained in good condition apart from a spate of gorse bushes and young trees', the notes for participants stated! In this photograph Worcester's ex-GWR 2-6-2T No 4571 is standing at the platform at Bromyard where a number of local passengers joined the train for the 13-mile journey to Leominster.**

Left **26 April 1958:** The first stop for the last train on the Bromyard-Leominster line was Rowden Mill, 2.75 miles from Bromyard. This station has since been converted into a house and received a British Heritage Award in 1989. No restrictions were placed on passengers alighting from the train only at the platform! The young trees can be seen growing in the nearest track.

Below **26 April 1958:** Fencote station, 5 miles from Bromyard, was the second stop for the special last train. As this track had been disused for more than 5 years the schedule for the journey from Bromyard was 30 minutes (with a 10-minute stop at Rowden Mill).

Above **26 April 1958: The final stop on the branch was Steens Bridge, 4 miles from Leominster.**

Below **26 April 1958: When the SLS special last train from Bromyard arrived at Leominster it drew into the disused platform that had been used by the Bromyard branch trains. Note the very unusual signal box high above the main platform.**

Above **26 April 1958: No 4571 has been turned ready to depart from Leominster with the SLS special. After having stopped at all stations on the outward journey, the return journey was non-stop in 35 minutes for the 13 miles.**

Below **8 May 1958: Earlswood is the summit of the North Warwickshire line from Stratford-upon-Avon to Tyseley. In this view ex-GWR 2-6-0 No 5333 has reached the summit with a coal train from South Wales.**

27 May 1958, using service trains			
Station	Arrive	Depart	Loco(s)
Pwllheli		10.25am	2233
Dovey Junction	1.08pm	1.20	75005
Moat Lane	2.18	2.45	46508
Three Cocks Junction	4.49	4.53	46518
Hereford	5.57	6.05	5377
Gloucester (Central)	7.24		
Gloucester (Eastgate)		7.58	44776
Birmingham (New Street)	9.18		

Below **27 May 1958: Ex-Great Western 'Manor' Class 4-6-0 No 7810** *Draycott Manor* **runs into Ross-on-Wye past Ross signal box with a Hereford-Gloucester train. The Monmouth branch diverged to the right behind the rear coach of the train. The plate on the signal box used the town name 'Ross' only, as it did not officially become Ross-on-Wye until 1931.**

Right **27 May 1958: Ex-LMS 4P 4-4-0 Compound No 41165 is signalled away from Gloucester (Eastgate) on an evening local between 7.30 and 8.00pm. I am not sure what train it is as I only stopped in Gloucester from 7.24pm, having arrived at Central from Hereford via Ross-on-Wye and leaving at 7.58 from Eastgate on an express to Birmingham New Street, after walking the long footbridge between the two stations.**

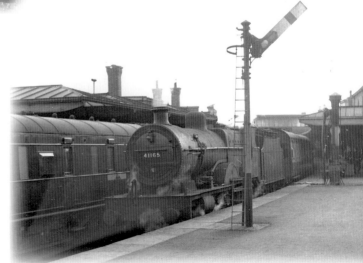

24 July 1958, using service trains			
Station	Arrive	Depart	Loco(s)
Birmingham (New Street)		9.23am	40489 to Gloucester
			45006
Berkeley Road	11.19	11.52	1430
Lydney Town	12.21pm		
Lydney Junction		1.18	4937
Grange Court Junction	1.41	2.19	4358
Ross-on-Wye	2.45	3.00	1456
Monmouth (Troy)	3.42	3.47	6439
Severn Tunnel Junction	4.50	5.17	4937
Newport	5.39		

Below **24 July 1958:** 'The Cornishman' rushes south through Berkeley Road, on the Gloucester to Bristol main line, hauled by 'Castle' Class 4-6-0 No 5028 *Llantilio Castle*. This express ran from Sheffield to Penzance and Paignton at this time.

Left **24 July 1958:** 0-4-2T No 1430 stands in the branch platform at Berkeley Road with the 11.52am train to Lydney Town via the Severn Bridge. On this warm day nearly all the droplight windows in the coach were lowered.

24 July 1958: Lydney Town was the terminus of the local train service on the remnant of the Severn & Wye Railway from Berkeley Road via Sharpness and the Severn Bridge. Ex-GWR 0-4-2T No 1430 is taking water at Lydney Junction after returning from Lydney Town, where it had arrived at 12.21pm with the 11.52am service from Berkeley Road.

Above **24 July 1958: Grange Court Junction was on the main line from Gloucester to South Wales, where the line to Ross-on-Wye and Hereford branched off. At 2.12pm 2-6-2T No 5156 arrives with 1.14pm Hereford to Gloucester train.**

Below **24 July 1958: At 2.19pm ex-GWR 2-6-0 No 4358 leaves the main line with the 2.05pm Gloucester to Hereford train. Grange Court station closed on 2 November 1964 when passenger services to Ross-on-Wye and Hereford were withdrawn, and the branch was finally closed and lifted after 1 November 1965.**

Left **24 July 1958: The Wye Valley branch trains to Monmouth used a bay platform at Ross-on-Wye, where 0-4-2T No 1456 waits to take the 3.00pm train to Monmouth. Collett 0-6-0 No 2248 has just brought the 2.25pm Hereford to Gloucester train into the through platform. Behind the coach of the Monmouth train by the tree on the extreme right of the picture can be seen Ross-on-Wye engine shed; this is now the only thing that remains from this scene, and is used as an antique showroom.**

Below **24 July 1958: At Monmouth (Troy) station ex-GWR 0-6-0PT No 6439 awaits departure at 3.47pm with the train down the Wye Valley to Chepstow.**

24 July 1958: Severn Tunnel Junction station was the destination of the 3.47pm train from Monmouth, which has arrived behind 0-6-0PT No 6439 of Newport (Ebbw Junction) shed.

Below 23 August 1958: Trains from the South Wales direction going forward from Gloucester towards Birmingham often received assistance from an additional locomotive. This morning BR 4-6-0 No 73155 is being assisted by ex-LMS Compound 4-4-0 No 41165, which was allocated to Bourneville shed at the time. This photograph was taken from end of the platform at Eastgate station. Note the coal-fired stove, which was used to keep the water in the water tower from freezing in winter.

23 August 1958, using service trains			
Station	Arrive	Depart	Loco(s)
Shirley		7.54am	DMU
Gloucester (Central)	9.36	11.30	1627
Cinderford	12.22pm	4.08	1627
Gloucester (Central)	4.49	6.24	4573
Ledbury Junction	7.19	8.33	DMU
Birmingham (Snow Hill)	10.01		

Above **23 August 1958:** 'Gloucester Passenger Stn' signal box provides the background to ex-LMS 2-6-0 No 42940 of Crewe South shed, which is on a train for Burton-upon-Trent via Birmingham (New Street). The train consists of ex-LMS coaches, the first three painted in the red and cream livery of early British Railways days.

Below **23 August 1958:** 'Super power' for the 2.15pm express from Paddington to Cheltenham is left at the platform at Gloucester (Central) as the train is pulled out on the last part of the journey to Cheltenham, probably by 0-6-0PT No 9441. The leading 'Castle' Class locomotive is No 5068 *Beverston Castle*, which appears to be in ex-works condition and was probably added at Swindon to train engine 'Castle' No 4085 *Berkeley Castle*. I have been told that No 5068 was the most camera-shy of the 'Castles', not many pictures having been published of it.

Left **23 August 1958: The crew of 2-6-2T No 4573 both get in the picture while waiting in the westbound bay with the 6.24pm stopping train to Ledbury Junction via Newent.**

Below **23 August 1958: 0-6-0PT No 1627 has just uncoupled from the 11.30am Gloucester to Cinderford train and is about to run round its coaches for the return journey. The station nameboard was unusual: it was a normal GWR-style board but was suspended from a timber frame, which was, I guess, a local Forest of Dean product.**

Above **23 August 1958: No 1627 has run round its two coaches and is reversing into the station to prepare for its return journey to Gloucester at 1.00pm. At the time this Saturdays-only train was the only departure down the branch to Newnham-on-Severn and Gloucester between 9.25am and 4.08pm.**

Centre **23 August 1958: The 1.00pm train prepares for its departure from Cinderford. Note the Ford Prefect parked in the station yard and the adverts extolling the virtues of Margate and telling you not to forget the ticket for your dog!**

Left **23 August 1958: A typical Great Western branch-line train at a beautiful country station – 2-6-2T No 4573 stands at Dymock station with the 6.24pm train from Gloucester (Central) to Ledbury Junction. The station platforms are tidy, the hedges on the left neatly clipped, and the milk churns neatly arranged on the station trolley – everything seems perfect, but the following year the station was closed and the passenger trains withdrawn.**

SLS Swindon Works special, 7 September 1958			
Station	**Arrive**	**Depart**	**Loco(s)**
Birmingham (Snow Hill)		9.15am	4900
Stratford-upon-Avon		9.56	
Gloucester (Central)	10.53	12.30	
Swindon Works	2.07	5.32	
Didcot	6.15	6.55	
Stratford-upon-Avon	8.20		
Birmingham (Snow Hill)	9.11		

Below 7 September 1958: During the late 1950s the Stephenson Locomotive Society (Midland Area) ran many special trains organised by the late W. A. Camwell, and I took part in a large number of them, which accounts for the numerous appearances of the 'SLS Special' headboard in the photographs I have included in this book. This view of Gloucester Horton Road (ex-Great Western) shed was taken from up a signal (with permission) at Gloucester Central. As this was a Sunday there were many more locomotives than normal in the yard, and the presence of the SLS special accounts for the large number of people roaming about.

Above **7 September 1958:** This picture was taken from the same signal post, but looking into the station. The special was from Birmingham (Snow Hill) to Swindon Works via Stratford-upon-Avon, visiting both Gloucester sheds and Didcot shed on the way out and back. The locomotive is 'Hall' Class 4-6-0 No 4900 *Saint Martin*, the prototype 'Hall' Class locomotive that was converted from a 'Saint' Class 4-6-0.

Right **7 September 1958:** The same train is seen from ground level. In the distance behind the water tower can be seen the cathedral tower, and crossing behind the water tower is the notorious long covered footbridge between Gloucester's Central and Eastgate stations.

Right 7 September 1958: 'WD' 2-8-0s were regular visitors to Gloucester on ironstone trains from the Banbury area to South Wales. No 90474 has been left in Horton Road shed yard in the normal filthy state of these engines.

Left 7 September 1958: Midland Railway Class 2P 4-4-0 No 40540 stands forlornly at the buffer stops just a few yards from the entrance to Gloucester (Bearwood) depot, hemmed in by other locomotives all more than 50 years old, Midland Railway 2F 0-6-0 No 58165 and 3F 0-6-0 No 43520.

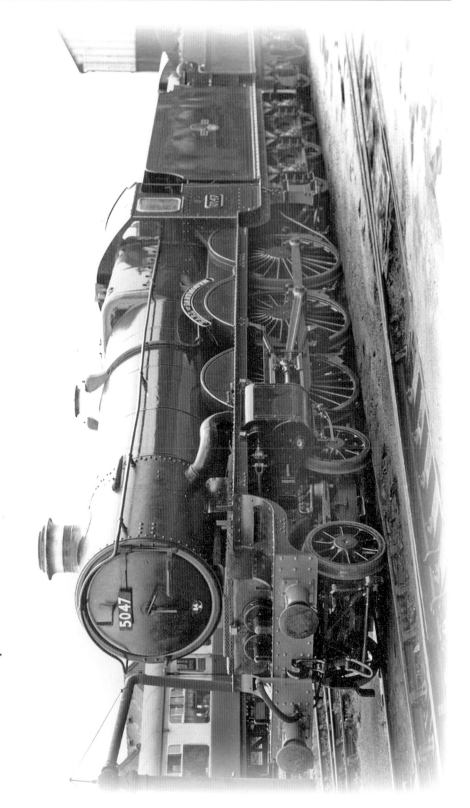

7 September 1958: An immaculate 'Castle' Class locomotive at Swindon Works. No 5047 *Earl of Dartmouth* was a Wolverhampton (Stafford Road) engine and as such often worked the Wolverhampton–Penzance 'Cornishman' train.

PUBLIC NOTICE

The British Transport Commission hereby give notice that on, and from Monday, 5th January, 1959 the passenger train service operating between Chepstow and Monmouth (Troy) will be withdrawn. Freight and parcels facilities will also be withdrawn from St. Briavels.

The following stations and halts will be completely closed:

TUTSHILL HALT (for Beachley)   ST. BRIAVELS
TIDENHAM HALT   WHITEBROOK HALT
NETHERHOPE HALT   PENALLT HALT
BROCKWEIR HALT   WYESHAM HALT
LLANDOGO HALT

Buses are operated in the area by Messrs. Red & White Services. Ltd.

Collection and Delivery arrangements for parcels and "goods smalls" traffic will continue to be provided in the area and facilities for the handing in or collection of such traffic by the public will also continue to be available at Chepstow, Tintern, Redbrook-on-Wye and Monmouth (Troy) stations.

Facilities for dealing with freight traffic in full truck loads, previously dealt with at St. Briavels, will be available at either Tintern or Redbrook-on-Wye.

Special arrangements have been made for passengers using the alternative bus services who wish to avail themselves of Passengers' Luggage in advance Facilities. Luggage will be accepted upon senders undertaking to obtain a railway ticket from the nearest main line station. Alternatively passengers can obtain their tickets in advance at Monmouth (Troy) or Chepstow stations for the purpose of sending luggage in advance.

Any further information required in respect of these arrangements can be obtained upon application to:
Mr. W. J. Hartnell, District Commercial Manager, Newport. Tel. No. Newport 58461 (Ext. 261). Station Masters at Chepstow. Tel. No. Chepstow 2170. Monmouth (Troy) Tel. No. Monmouth 24.

SLS special last train, Chepstow-Monmouth-Ross-on-Wye-Chepstow, 4 January 1959			
Station	Arrive	Depart	Loco(s)
Chepstow		11.20am	6412, 6439
Tintern	11.35	11.45	
Redbrook-on-Wye	12.05pm	12.15	
Monmouth (Troy)	12.22	12.40	
Symonds Yat	12.55	1.05	
Lydbrook Junction	1.10	1.20	
Ross-on-Wye	1.36	1.55	
Monmouth (Troy)	2.15	2.30	
Chepstow	3.13	3.20	
Caldicot Junction	3.30	3.40	
Sudbrook Pumping Station	3.50	5.10	
(to visit steam beam engines)			
Severn Tunnel Junction	5.25		

Top left The death certificate of the Wye Valley service between Chepstow and Monmouth Troy.

Left 4 January 1959: A large crowd has gathered around 0-6-0PT No 6412 after arrival at Symonds Yat, where a local hotel provided farewell drinks to staff on the last train to call there. Many of the people in the photograph were local residents who turned out on this cold Sunday morning to say farewell.

Left **4 January 1959: Another view of the last train at Symonds Yat. 0-6-0PT No 6439, at the other end of the train, is out of sight at the far end of the station.**

Below left **4 January 1959: 0-6-0PT No 6439, also seen at Ross-on-Wye station, was on the rear of the train and carried tail lamps.**

Below right **4 January 1959: A general view of Ross-on-Wye station after the arrival of the last train on the Wye Valley line. The station was quite a large complex, all traces of which have now disappeared, but the new station at Kidderminster Town on the Severn Valley Railway is a copy of the main Ross station buildings.**

Above **4 January 1959:** The last train on the Wye Valley lines has crossed to the other platform at Ross ready to return to Monmouth and Chepstow. The train consisted of seven coaches topped and tailed by pannier tanks, each with a different headboard for the last trains from Monmouth to Chepstow and Monmouth to Ross, which were swapped around depending on which engine was leading on each line.

4 January 1959: At the end of the day in failing light, the last train on the Wye Valley lines paid a visit to the Severn Tunnel's Sudbrook Pumping Station, where visits had been arranged to inspect the steam beam engines that were still working pumping out the water from the tunnel. These were soon to be electrified.

7 March 1959, using service trains			
Station	Arrive	Depart	Loco(s)
Kings Norton		8.40am	43049
Ashchurch	10.21	11.15	41900
Upton-on-Severn	11.52	1.30pm	41900
Ashchurch	1.48	2.17	43049
Kings Norton	3.56		

Left 7 March 1959: Ashchurch was a complex junction at the time that this photograph was taken. The former Midland Railway Birmingham to Bristol main line is on the left of the picture, while ex-Midland 3F 0-6-0 No 43645 is standing on the Upton-on-Severn branch astride the access to the station platform. On the extreme left, out of the picture, is the line to Evesham and Redditch.

Above **7 March 1959: On this very wet day ex-LMS 2-6-0 No 43049 stands in the Redditch line platform at Ashchurch having arrived with the 8.27am local from Birmingham (New Street) via Evesham.**

Below **7 March 1959: The old Midland Railway signal box at Ashchurch has been replaced by a new BR-designed one. Note the empty stock of the 8:27am from Birmingham (New Street) standing behind the new box. This stock stood at Ashchurch from 10.21am until 2.25pm, when it returned to Birmingham.**

Above **7 March 1959: A northbound express rushes through Ashchurch hauled by Midland 2P 4-4-0 No 40489 and 'Jubilee' 4-6-0 No 45609** *Gilbert and Ellice Islands*. **The train is possibly the 8.30am Cardiff to Newcastle express, which often took a pilot loco from Gloucester to Birmingham (see also page 53). The station nameboard mentions that it is the junction for Tewksbury, Evesham, Alcester and Redditch. The Tewksbury and Upton-on-Severn train left from the other side of the building behind the train.**

Below **7 March 1959: On that day the Upton-on-Severn branch was being worked by ex-Midland 0-4-4T No 41900, seen here leaving its single coach after arriving from Tewkesbury with the Saturdays-only 11.00am Tewkesbury to Ashchurch train. Immediately behind the buildings, adjacent to the platform with the canopy, is the main line from Bristol to Birmingham, with the curved platform used by Evesham trains on the extreme right.**

Left **7 March 1959: The coach for the 11.15am Ashchurch to Upton-on-Severn train stands in the platform at Ashchurch while No 41900 runs round it.**

Below **7 March 1959: Ready to depart from Ashchurch – the crew were quite prepared to wait for me to take the photograph as I was the only passenger.**

Left 7 **March 1959: Ex-MR 0-4-4T No 41900 stands at Tewkesbury station with the 11.15am train from Ashchurch to Upton-on-Severn.**

Below **7 March 1959: Between Tewksbury and Upton-on-Severn was the little country station of Ripple, where No 41900 waits for the departure time of 11.31am. As I was the only passenger there was no need to hurry.**

Above **7 March 1959:** Upton-on-Severn was the terminus of the line from Ashchurch; the line on to Malvern Wells had been closed since 1952, and this stump was to close on 14 August 1961. No 41900 had arrived at 11.52 with its one passenger.

Below **7 March 1959:** At the very end of the Upton-on-Severn branch, No 41900 has pulled forward into the headshunt while the fireman changes the points to allow it to run round the one coach and take it back to Ashchurch at 1.30pm, leaving plenty of time for a leisurely lunch. The return journey again had me as its solitary passenger – the only occasion I have had my own private train on a branch line!

SLS Birmingham area tour, 30 May 1959			
Station	Arrive	Depart	Loco(s)
Birmingham (New Street)		1.20pm	58271, 58283
Harborne	1.32	1.50	
Smethwick Galton Junction	2.24	2.26	
Old Hill	(2.39)		
Halesowen	2.45	2.50	
Longbridge	3.02	3.07	
Camp Hill	(3.22)		
Birmingham (New Street)			

0-6-0s Nos 58271 and 58283. The reason for the very light locomotives was that later in the tour the train traversed the Old Hill to Halesowen branch, which included the very weight-restricted Dowery Dell Viaduct near Hunnington. This general view of Harborne station (closed on 26 November 1934) shows that the coal yard was still operational. Steps were provided to assist passengers down onto the track – the train was not run into the platform as it was leased to a company as a timber store and it was not considered safe to alight there, so detraining was by the safe alternative of climbing down on to the track. How times change!

Below **30 May 1959: On this Saturday the Stephenson Locomotive Society (Midland Area) ran its 'Golden Jubilee Birmingham Area Railtour', which visited Harborne as part of its route. On the Harborne branch the train was top and tailed by outward-facing ex-MR 2F**

Above **30 May 1959: No 58271 is prepared to return the train to the Birmingham (New Street) to Wolverhampton line at Harborne Junction, just a quarter of a mile from its home shed at Monument Lane.**

Right **30 May 1959: The disused Halesowen station (closed in 1927) was visited by the SLS special. Although closed for more than 30 years, when the station was inspected for use by the train the nameboard was found intact face-down in the weeds, so it was propped up for photographic purposes.**

The train encountered yet a third MR 0-6-0, No 58167, standing in the other platform allegedly 'just in case of problems'. The station buildings were still in use as goods offices for traffic generated by local industry.

30 May 1959: Surrounded by the Longbridge Works of the British Motor Corporation (Austin), Longbridge station was also visited by the rail tour. After this stop the train returned to Birmingham (New Street) via Camp Hill, where the participants changed trains into a DMU – the first rail tour to use one of these sets.

Above 28 July 1959: This is the view from the north end of Platform 5 at Birmingham (Snow Hill) station on 'Hall' Class 4-6-0 No 4982 *Acton Hall* takes the centre track with a short freight from the Worcester line. Snow Hill North signal box was still in use at that time, although new electric signals were in place.

Below 1 August 1959: The very steep start from the platform at Stratford-upon-Avon up to Wilmcote necessitated the attachment of assisting locomotives to trains to Birmingham. On summer Saturdays the demand for assisting locomotives was very heavy and resulted in Collett 0-6-0s of the '2251' Class being coupled behind 'Castles' to provide the assistance; after the train had topped the summit of the line at Earlswood, the 'Castle' and its train would rush down the line to Tyseley with the crew of the '2251' holding on! This was the situation on this day when 'Castle' Class 4-6-0 No 5074 *Hampden* had assistance from 0-6-0 No 2211, seen here near the summit at Earlswood with the 11.15am Newquay to Wolverhampton train, which was one of the most notorious timekeepers on summer Saturdays.

Station	Arrive	Depart	Loco(s)
Bristol (Temple Meads)		12.15pm	9769
Canon's Marsh Goods Station	1.18	1.30	
Bristol (Temple Meads) Goods HL	2.15	2.23	
Avonside Wharf	2.34	2.36	
St Philips station	2.47	2.50	
Fishponds	3.00	3.10	
Clifton Down	3.25	3.32	
Yate	4.16	4.18	
Thornbury	4.40	4.55	
Berkeley Loop Junction	5.53	5.55	
Berkeley Road	6.00	6.03	
Mangotsfield	6.32		
Bristol (Temple Meads)	6.43		

RCTS Bristol and South Gloucestershire rail tour, 26 September 1959 (abbreviated itinerary)

Below **26 September 1959: The Railway Correspondence & Travel Society rail tour of Bristol and South Gloucestershire traversed the freight-only branch to Canon's Marsh Goods Station. No passenger train had ever previously traversed this sharply curved line. 0-6-0PT No 9769 is about to run round the train at the end of the branch.**

Above **26 September 1959:** The branch line to Thornbury from Yate, on the Midland main line from Bristol to Gloucester, was opened on 2 September 1872 and closed to passengers on 19 June

1944. No 9769 had just arrived at Thornbury with the three-coach RCTS special at about 4.40pm, and is about to uncouple to run round its train.

Below **26 September 1959:** No 9769 has pulled into the headshunt and is now running back to pass the coaches left in platform at Thornbury.

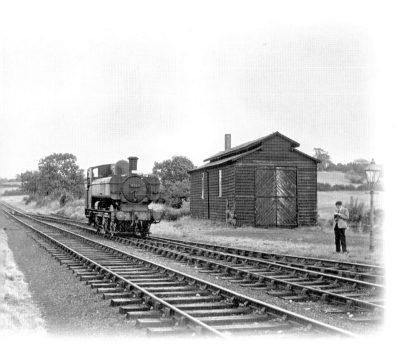

Above 26 September 1959: The tiny engine shed at Thornbury was still standing. The Midland Railway gas lamp on the right originally lit the shed yard.

Below 26 September 1959: No 9769 takes water at the enormous water tower that supplied the station and engine shed. A major part of the branch is still open as far as Tytherington Quarry, but the section to Thornbury closed completely on 30 September 1967.

1960

5 March 1960, using service trains			
Station	**Arrive**	**Depart**	**Loco(s)**
Shirley		7.54am	DMU
Stratford-upon-Avon	8.34	9.05	?
Honeybourne	9.25	9.40	8488
Cheltenham Spa St James	10.36	12.15pm	4573
Kingham	1.08	1.40	4573
Andoversford Junction	2.15*	2.14*	31619
Savernake (Low Level)	3.59		
(continuation not remembered or recorded)			
* Scheduled times, but connection was usually made!			

Below **5 March 1960: Busy days at Honeybourne Junction, with the beautiful Great Western nameboard in front of Collett 0-6-0s Nos 2273 and 3204.**

Below **5 March 1960:** The station nameboard needed altering the day after this photograph was taken of 0-6-0PT No 8488 on the 9.40am local train to Cheltenham – it was the last day of this service, and Broadway, Winchcombe and Cheltenham would have to be deleted. The station closed in 1969 and was demolished, but in 1985 a single platform with 'bus shelter' was reopened for the Cotswold Line service.

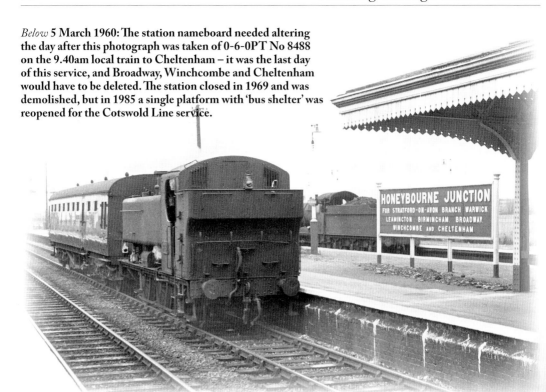

Below **5 March 1960:** 0-6-0PT No 8488 calls at Winchcombe with the 9.40am Honeybourne to Cheltenham Spa (St James) local train on the last day of the service, and the day the station closed, only to be reopened by the Gloucestershire Warwickshire Railway in the 1980s.

Right **5 March 1960: Notgrove was on the line from Cheltenham to Andoversford and Kingham, and was the summit of the branch over the Cotswolds. Ex-GWR 2-6-2T No 4573 waits to depart with the 12.15pm Cheltenham Spa (St James) to Kingham train at 12.45pm.**

Below **5 March 1960: Two Kingham branch trains pass at Bourton-on-the-Water – 2-6-2T No 4573 is on the 12:.15pm Cheltenham to Kingham train, passing 2-6-2T No 5173 on a Kingham to Cheltenham service. By utilising a Paddington to Worcester service, connecting with the branch trains at Kingham, a quieter journey from London to Cheltenham could be made than by travelling on the more familiar route via Swindon and Gloucester.**

5 March 1960: Back at Andoversford (always shown as Andoversford Junction in the timetable), the 1.56pm Cheltenham to Andover Junction train is arriving. This was the only train of the day from here to Andover and was scheduled to depart at 2.14pm. A service from Kingham was scheduled to arrive at 2.15pm, and is signalled away towards Cheltenham in this photograph.

Below left: **19 April 1960:** Diesel railbuses were used to operate services on two branch lines from Kemble. This is Tetbury, the terminus of one of them.

Above: **19 April 1960:** Cirencester (Town) station was at the end of the other branch. The branch railbus is waiting to depart for Kemble.

Below: **5 March 1960:** This is the 'other' Swindon station, Swindon Town on the Cheltenham to Andover Junction line, which saw one through train in each direction per day together with three or four local trains. Ex-SR 2-6-0 No 31619 receives a drop of oil while waiting with the 1.56pm Cheltenham to Andover Junction train at 3.19pm.

Above 6 August 1960: Summer Saturdays serious stretched locomotive availability in the late 1950s and early 1960s, and on this day the situation must have been desperate, as this view at Churchdown shows. The train is 1N86, the 8.05am Newquay to Newcastle, running 47 minutes late and hauled by ex-LMS 4F 0-6-0 No 44296 and BR 2-10-0 No 92137. Churchdown station was closed on 2 November 1964, but proposals have been made to reopen it at some time in the future.

Right 9 August 1960: The transport of iron ore from the East Midlands to South Wales created a lot of traffic in the early 1960s. The trains ran on the former Stratford-upon-Avon & Midland Junction Railway to Stratford, where they joined the former Great Western line to travel to South Wales via Cheltenham and Gloucester. One of these trains is seen here heading towards Gloucester at The Reddings; just beyond the road bridge behind the train is the site of Hatherley Junction.

Above **13 August 1960: Ex-LMS 0-6-0 No 44209 has just arrived at Platform 9 of Birmingham (New Street) station on a Saturday stopping train from Gloucester. The public thoroughfare across the station is clearly visible in the background.**

Right **13 August 1960: The sun penetrates the gloom of Birmingham (New Street) and illuminates the boiler and smokebox of 'Jubilee' 4-6-0 No 45660 *Rooke* on train M214, the 7.40am Bristol to Bradford, waiting to depart from Platform 7.**

Left 13 August 1960: Leaving Platform 10 of New Street station with train M245, the 7.40am Bradford to Bournemouth, is ex-LMS 4-6-0 No 44983, a Leeds engine.

Below 13 August 1960: BR Standard 4-6-0 No 73136 (one of the group with Caprotti valve-gear) stands at Platform 8 at New Street with a train from the West of England ready to proceed forward towards Derby.

Interlude: The Severn Bridge, 1956-67

Above **Before the Severn Tunnel was opened in 1885 the Severn & Wye Railway's Severn Bridge was the lowest crossing of the River Severn. The bridge was opened in 1879 from near Lydney to Sharpness, and this picture was taken in August 1956 from the window of a train between Lydney and Gloucester looking south-west down the estuary.**

Left **This unusual view of the Severn Bridge was taken from the footplate of the locomotive on a Sharpness to Lydney train approaching the Lydney end of the bridge. To the right of the track can be seen the gas main from Sharpness to Lydney.**

Above On night of 25 October 1960, in dense fog at about 10.30pm, two loaded oil tankers on their way from the refinery collided near the entrance to Sharpness Docks, drifted upstream on the tide and hit the pier between spans 19 and 20, which brought down the spars and fractured the gas main, causing an explosion and fire. At first plans were prepared to repair the bridge, but ultimately it was decided to demolish it.

Main picture The gap caused by the accident can clearly be seen in this view of the bridge taken in March 1961 from a train travelling between Gloucester and Lydney.

Below In August 1967 demolition of the Severn Bridge is taking place, as seen from the towpath of the Gloucester & Sharpness Canal, which ran parallel with the east bank of the river. The large crane was the *Magnus II* from Hamburg, which was hired for the work.

Left **During the bridge demolition contract, the opening span over the Gloucester & Sharpness Canal was restored to working order and closed across the canal during working hours to enable access to the bridge.**

Centre **The cabin on top of the girders of the swinging span of the bridge was the signal box and engine house, and contained a compound steam engine and coal-fired boiler. The signalman was designated signalman/engine driver, and one of the men was re-employed to operate the bridge for the demolition contractors. He was very pleased to receive visitors to break the monotony of looking after a deserted signal box and only being required to keep the steam pressure up to operate the compound steam engine whenever a large vessel required the bridge to swing through 90 degrees and to open the bridge for canal traffic at the end of the working day.**

During the demolition contract the bridge was closed across the canal to enable the workmen to have access to the bridge. This is the view was from the signal box/engine house window.

Above **Signs on either side of the swingbridge instructed shipping to blow three long blasts if they required the bridge to be swung open. A fleet of oil tankers plied the Gloucester & Sharpness Canal, and the *Waterdale H* has passed through the opened span during the demolition contract in August 1967 on its way empty from Gloucester to Sharpness, then out into the estuary and down to the oil refinery. The two tankers of the same type that collided with the bridge were *Arkendale H* and *Wastdale H*. Access to the cabin when the bridge was open to canal traffic was via a staircase within the tower, and access to the tower was along the towpath.**

Right **This is the view from the signal box/ engine house after the bridge had been swung open at the end of the working day, showing the view along the canal and estuary towards Sharpness Docks. At the end of the day the demolition workmen could leave the bridge across the closed swinging span and walk through the cutting at the end of the bridge to go home, but the engineman had to climb down the tower steps and go home along the towpath.**

1961

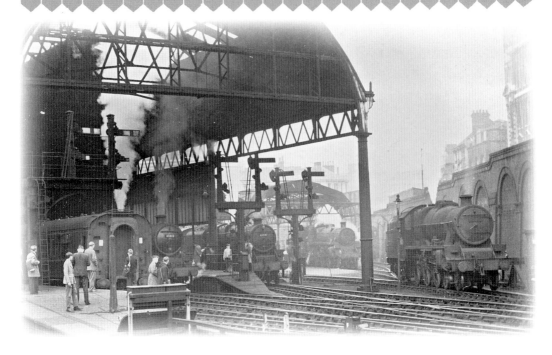

Above **15 April 1961: On the former Midland Railway side of Birmingham (New Street) station an array of locomotives wait to take trains westward.**

SLS Severn & Wye District tour, 13 May 1961 (abbreviated itinerary)			
Station	**Arrive**	**Depart**	**Loco(s)**
Gloucester Central		2.15	
Bullo Pill	2.33	2.34	
Cinderford	2.57	3.10	6437
Northern United Sidings	3.30	3.35	
Bullo Pill	4.05	4.10	
Lydney Town	4.42	4.50	
Coleford Junction	5.00	5.05	8701
Coleford	5.17	5.30	
Coleford Junction	(5.43)		
Serridge Junction	6.05	6.15	
Coleford Junction	(6.36)		
Lydney Junction	7.14	7.20	
Gloucester (Central)	7.50		

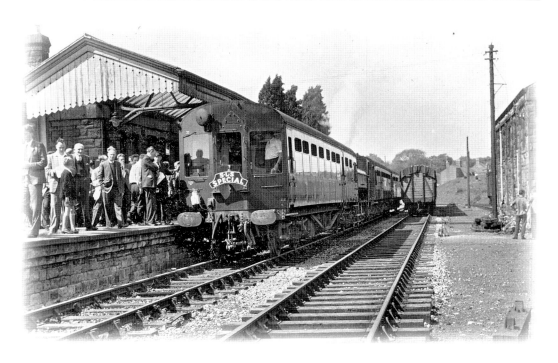

Above **13 May 1961: This Stephenson Locomotive Society rail tour covered of most the lines remaining in the Forest of Dean. The push-pull formation was coach-loco-two coaches; all the push-pull apparatus was in working order and the retractable coach steps also worked, which enabled numerous photo stops to be made. At this stop in Cinderford station at 3.00pm the steps were not needed.**

Below **13 May 1961: Another view of the SLS special at Cinderford. Ex-GWR 0-6-0PT No 6437 is in fully lined green livery.**

Below **13 May 1961:** After leaving Cinderford the rail tour visited the Northern United Colliery, the last main underground colliery to close in the Forest of Dean, leaving only small 'free mines' operational. The tour participants are moving around the track and in the driving compartment of the coach. The steps on the nearest coach were opened on the opposite side, but on the first coach beyond the loco they are out on this side. Not a pair of jeans in sight!

Below **13 May 1961:** At Coleford Junction the very steeply graded line to Coleford left the Parkend to Serridge Junction line. Due to the heavy gradient at 1 in 30 and 1 in 31 most of the way additional power was provided by 0-6-0PT No 8701, which inherited the 'SLS Special' headboard as it would lead the unusual procession up the branch. At the small signal box in the distance it was 'open house' to any tour participants who wished to visit.

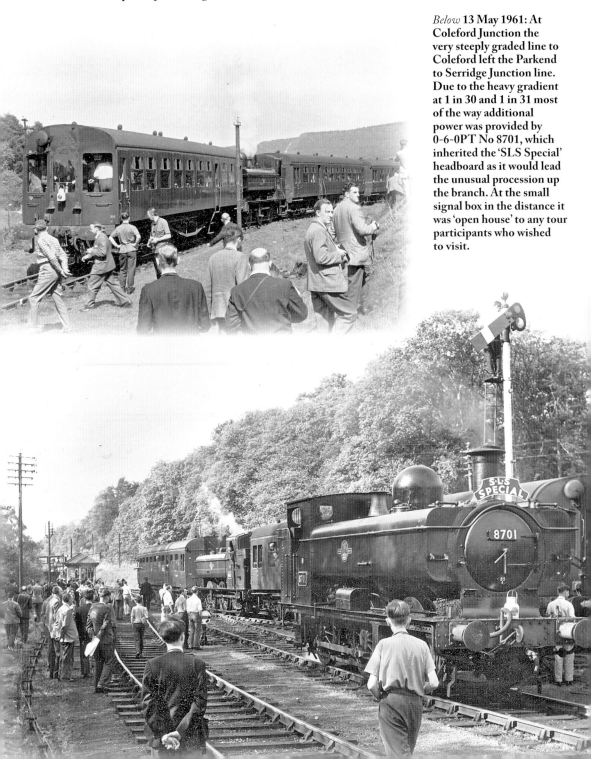

Above **13 May 1961:** The SLS rail tour of the Forest of Dean is seen at Coleford (S&WJR) station, the first for many years as passenger services were withdrawn in July 1929. After the fierce 3-mile climb up the branch, the last quarter of a mile was down into the station at 1 in 47. At this time the line ahead of the train continued into Coleford GWR station and on to Whitecliff Siding; until 1917 the line continued to Monmouth. Ready to depart for its return to Coleford Junction at 5.30pm, the headboard is at the other end; No 8701 is fitted with two tail lamps, while No 6437 in the middle of the train is ready to push and pull.

Below **13 May 1961:** Deep in the forest on the main Lydney-Cinderford line, Serridge Junction was once the junction for the line to Lydbrook Junction, but by this date there had been no traffic for a long while, as the line to Lydbrook had closed in January 1956 and the Cinderford line via Drybrook Road in 1929. The SLS rail tour travelled to this remote point, and due to the steps at the doors of the auto-coaches passengers were able to climb out and explore the area during a 10-minute stop on this lovely evening.

27 May 1961: A National Railway Museum locomotive, former Midland Railway Compound 4-4-0 No 1000 was chartered by the Gloucestershire Railway Society for a special train from Gloucester to Derby and return. The outward journey was via the Ashchurch–Evesham–Redditch line and the return was via the Stratford-upon-Avon & Midland Junction line from Blisworth to Stratford-upon-Avon. The return leg was routed over the new east-to-south chord that joined the S&MJR to the former GWR Stratford-upon-Avon to Cheltenham line, constructed for the use of iron ore trains from the East Midlands to South Wales. This photograph shows the train standing at Stratford-upon-Avon (Old Town) station at 8.45pm. The station had closed to passenger trains on 7 April 1952 after 76 years of use.

27 May 1961: Two imposing views showing the sleek lines of No 1000 standing on the new chord line at Stratford-upon-Avon.

3 June 1961, using service trains			
Station	Arrive	Depart	Loco(s)
Gloucester (Central)	12.48pm	6348	
Hereford	1.57	3.00	DMU
Leominster	3.22	3.50	1445
Ludlow	4.09	4.15	1445
Woofferton	4.25	4.30	1445
Tenbury Wells	4.40	4.58	W24W
Bewdley	5.32	5.57	DMU
Birmingham (Snow Hill)	7.31		
The same itinerary with the same locos was repeated on 24 June 1961, but omitting Woofferton-Ludlow Woofferton, and between Tenbury Wells and Bewdley the railcar was W23W.			

Below **3 June 1961: Ex-GWR 4-6-0 No 5952** *Cogan Hall* **is stand-by engine and station pilot at Hereford, standing on the centre track with a single parcels van. On the right 2-6-0 No 6348 is arriving with the 12.48pm train from Gloucester at about 2.00pm.**

Above 3 June 1961: Ex-GWR 0-4-2T No 1445 waits in the branch-line platform at Leominster with the 3.50pm local train to Ludlow, while a DMU trains stands in the main-line platform with a Hereford to Shrewsbury train, due to leave at 3.22pm. The unusual signal box dominates the picture – from the platform an excellent view could be had of the interlocking mechanisms operating as the various levers were pulled. The girders crossing above the branch train were part of the structure of the signal box to give it stability.

Left **3 June 1961: Ludlow was the terminus for the 3.50pm service from Hereford, hauled by ex-GWR 0-4-2T No 1445. The train will change platforms to become the 4.15pm to Tenbury Wells, running in coach-first formation to Woofferton, where it will reverse.**

Below **3 June 1961: Leominster shed was a sub-shed to Hereford, and that afternoon the residents were Collett 0-6-0 No 2242 and a '5700' Class 0-6-0 pannier tank waiting for their next duties. Both are well coaled, demonstrating the need for the bars on the pannier's rear windows.**

Right **24 June 1961:** The same itinerary with much the same locos was followed again three weeks later (see the table on page 96). Fawley was a passing station between Ross-on-Wye and Hereford on the Gloucester to Hereford line, and in the early afternoon ex-GWR 2-6-0 No 6348 waits with the 12.40pm Gloucester to Hereford train for the arrival of 2-6-2T No 4115 with a Hereford to Gloucester service. This must be as near as possible to a 'sun directly overhead' photo as it is possible to take in England – 1.30pm BST on Midsummer Day!

Below right **24 June 1961:** The north-to-west LMS & GWR Joint line from Shrewsbury to Newport carried important expresses from the West of England to North West England. In the summer of 1961 the ex-GWR 'King' Class locomotives had been ousted from many of the expresses on the Bristol, South Wales and West of England main lines to London by the new diesels, and were available to work trains through Hereford. Here 'King' Class 4-6-0 No 6018 *King Henry VI* waits for the signals to clear for its 2.55pm departure northwards from Hereford with the 11.50am Swansea to Manchester (London Road) train.

Right **24 June 1961:
Woofferton, on the
Hereford to Shrewsbury
line, was the junction for
the Wyre Forest branch to
Bewdley. Ex-GWR
0-4-2T No 1445 waits
with the 4.00pm train to
Ludlow, the next station
north on the main line to
Shrewsbury.**

Below **24 June 1961: No
1445 arrives back at
Woofferton Junction
propelling the 4.15pm
service from Ludlow, and is
scheduled to go down the
branch to Tenbury Wells at
4.30pm. The branch can be
seen leaving the main line in
front of the signal box.**

Above **24 June 1961:**
No 1445 is ready to go
forward again from
Woofferton Junction
as the 4.30pm train to
Tenbury Wells.

Right **24 June 1961:**
Tenbury Wells is the
terminus for the 4.15pm
train from Ludlow. The
train will later leave to
return to Woofferton,
then north along the main
line to Craven Arms,
finally returning south to
Leominster.

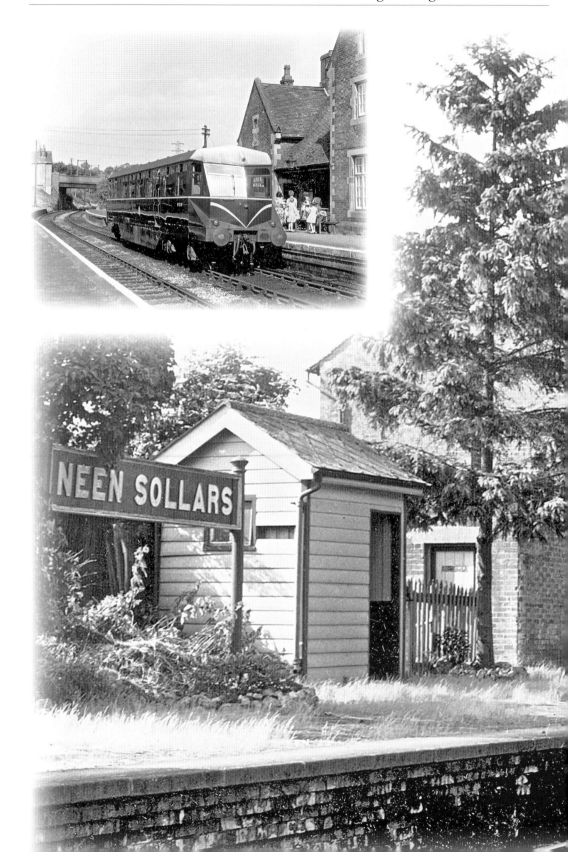

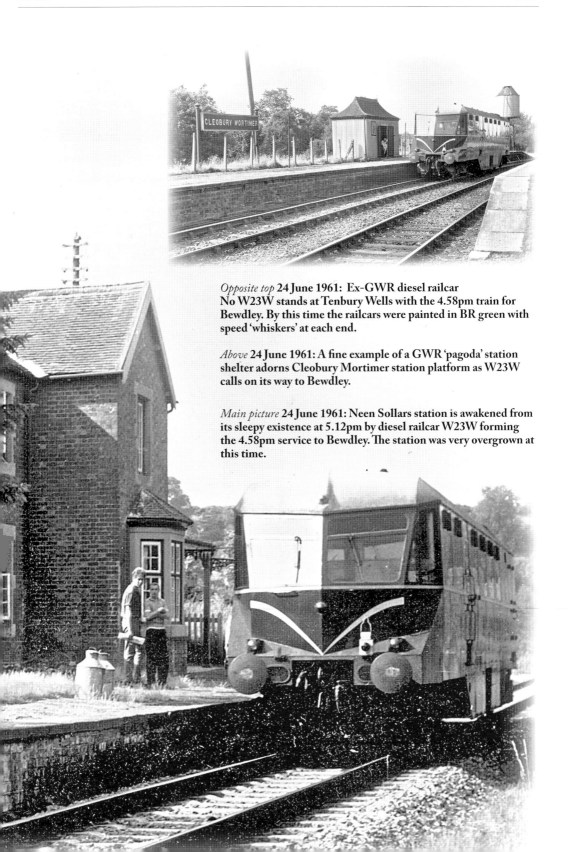

Opposite top **24 June 1961: Ex-GWR diesel railcar No W23W stands at Tenbury Wells with the 4.58pm train for Bewdley. By this time the railcars were painted in BR green with speed 'whiskers' at each end.**

Above **24 June 1961: A fine example of a GWR 'pagoda' station shelter adorns Cleobury Mortimer station platform as W23W calls on its way to Bewdley.**

Main picture **24 June 1961: Neen Sollars station is awakened from its sleepy existence at 5.12pm by diesel railcar W23W forming the 4.58pm service to Bewdley. The station was very overgrown at this time.**

1962

Above Late summer 1962: Until 10 September 1962 a passenger train service was operated from Coaley Junction, between Yate and Standish Junction, and the market town of Dursley. Many classes of light engines saw out their twilight years of service here, and this photograph, taken at Coaley Junction, shows the Dursley train waiting to depart after the arrival of a main-line train from Gloucester, which is standing at the platform behind it. One coach was the normal consist of the train and was more than adequate. The locomotive is ex-Midland Railway 3F 0-6-0 No 43593. The station closed on 4 January 1965, but in 1995 a new station was opened just north of this one, called Cam & Dursley.

Opposite top Late summer 1962: The train from Coaley Junction has arrived at Dursley. The photographic possibilities of this station were extremely limited after the train had stopped, and this was the only angle possible from the middle of the road outside.

Opposite bottom Late summer 1962: The station at Dursley was very cramped and sandwiched between factories, which produced some freight traffic. On this day the returning branch train had two goods vans and a brake-van attached, and the pigeons in the baskets on the platform were the only occupants of the coach other than myself.

Above **October 1962: BR LMR 2-6-0 No 46510 stands with a Hereford to Three Cocks Junction train at Hay-on-Wye, at that time an unspoiled Midland Railway station.** This photograph is strictly outside the 'Cathedral Counties', being situated in Wales just across the River Wye from Herefordshire.

Below **October 1962: Three Cocks Junction was a fascinating place.** The former Midland Railway branch line from Hereford joined the former Cambrian Railways Mid Wales line from Moat Lane via Builth, then they ran as a joint line to Talyllyn Junction, where it joined the Brecon & Merthyr, then on to Brecon, where it joined the Neath & Brecon. The train from Hereford behind No 46510 has terminated at Three Cocks Junction, to connect with a Moat Lane to Brecon train; after a wait of about half an hour it will return to Hereford.

Above **October 1962:** The train from Hereford is in the process of changing platforms. The station had a refreshment room, which always seemed to be open although it was empty whenever I ended up there. I always seemed to have a long wait whichever route I took through.

Below **October 1962:** Sister engine BR LMR 2-6-0 No 46520 arrives at Three Cocks Junction from Moat Lane Junction via Rhayader and Builth, having followed the River Wye for a large part of its journey. Here it connected with the train from Hereford.

1963

Below 6 April 1963: In this general view of the north end of Gloucester (Central) station, the train entering the station is hauled by large 'Prairie' 2-6-2T No 6137, originally built for Paddington suburban services. At the time of this photograph the London services had been dieselised and the engine was reallocated to Gloucester (Horton Road) depot, to work out its final years on local services around the city. Behind the last coach is Gloucester East signal box, which controlled the northern end of Central station, in the distance can be discerned a train standing in Gloucester (Eastgate) station.

6 April 1963, using service trains			
Station	Arrive	Depart	Loco(s)
Downfield Crossing Halt		3.23pm	1472
Gloucester (Central)	3.49	5.15	1453
Chalford	5.57	6.03	1453
Downfield Crossing Halt	6.21		

Above **6 April 1963: A 'loco portrait' of ex-GWR 0-4-2T No 1472 standing in the north bay at Central station on Chalford 'Auto' duties; on this occasion the engine was running round its local coach at each end of the journey.**

Left **6 April 1963: Sister engine No 1453 (with home-made smokebox number plate) is also seen in the north bay at Central station with an 'auto-train' for Chalford in the Stroud Valley. The 85B plate at the base of the smokebox indicates that the locomotive is from Horton Road depot, Gloucester.**

Above **6 April 1963: Arriving at Chalford after the journey up the Stroud Valley, passengers alighted at the far platform and the train pulled forward to a siding on the up side of the line until the down line was free, then proceeded into the down platform *(below)* to await departure time for the return down the valley. No 1453 propels the train into the platform to become the 6.03pm departure for Cheltenham. The station was still lit by gas at this time.**

Above **6 April 1963: Inside the 'auto-coach' being propelled by No 1453 – the standing passenger hanging straps were not required on this trip!**

Above 6 April 1963: Having alighted from the train at Downfield Crossing Halt at 6.21pm I photographed No 1453 propelling the 6.03pm Chalford to Gloucester 'auto-train' towards Gloucester.

Below 6 April 1963: I then photographed BR(W) 'Castle' Class 4-6-0 No 7006 *Lydford Castle* storming up the bank between Stonehouse and Stroud with a Cheltenham to Paddington express. Note the paraffin lamps on the extreme left and next to the station nameboard on the right. Passengers crossed from one platform to the other using the board crossing under the loco's tender in this photograph; when trains approached from either direction a bell sounded to warn anyone about to use the crossing. This train was the 5.45pm Cheltenham (St James) to Paddington express, due at Stroud (the next stop) at 6.36pm.

Left **July 1963:** This Chalford 'auto-train' has been strengthened to two trailers, and is being propelled by ex-GWR 0-4-2T No 1472 towards Gloucester. This stretch of line was the fastest on the run from Chalford to Gloucester and often, especially at around 8.00am, the Chalford-Gloucester train in 'push' mode would overtake a Midland-line northbound express, which would be slowing for the curve at Tuffley Junction, to the consternation of passengers on the express!

Below **July 1963:** A Chalford 'auto-train' engine on the loose – 0-4-2T No 1409 is heading out of Gloucester on the ex-LMS line, which means it is not going to the Stroud Valley, as it was not possible to cross from the LMS lines to the GWR lines in this direction at Standish Junction. The only assumption is that it was heading for Berkeley Road to work the Sharpness service.

Left **July 1963: Seen from the same public footpath crossing near Tuffley, LMS 'Jubilee' 4-6-0 No 45709** *Implacable* **approaches Gloucester with the summer Saturday 2.15pm Bristol to York train.**

Centre **July 1963: Ex-GWR 'Grange' Class 4-6-0 No 6828** *Trellech Grange* **heads towards Gloucester on the former Great Western lines. This train will avoid Gloucester station on the Gloucester South (now known as Yard Junction) to Engine Shed Junction line.**

Bottom **July 1963: Relegated to a ballast train, ex-GWR 'Hall' Class 4-6-0 No 4992** *Crosby Hall*, **with a large-capacity tender, heads out of Gloucester.**

1964

Left **22 August 1964: Very grimy 'Manor' Class 4-6-0 No 7814** *Fringford Manor*, **which has lost its smokebox number plate and has only received a replacement chalk number on its buffer beam, stands on the centre through road at Gloucester (Central). The day these photographs were taken I had just bought a second-hand 4 x 4 Rolleiflex camera and visited the station to try it out – these were the first results.**

22 August 1964: Central, the former Great Western station in Gloucester, is situated on the line from Tramway Junction, across the Severn and down the west bank, which was the main line from London to South Wales before the Severn Tunnel was completed. In steam days there were numerous freight trains on this line. This train appears to be a stone train, possibly from Tidenham Quarry in the Wye Valley, with a general goods train attached to the rear. Ex-GWR heavy freight 2-8-0T No 5252 from Aberdare drifts down the slope from the bridge over the River Severn on the through road. The platform and canopy behind the engine are still in use as Platform 4 of today's Gloucester station, but the buildings behind have long since disappeared, together with their ornamental wrought-ironwork on the roofs.

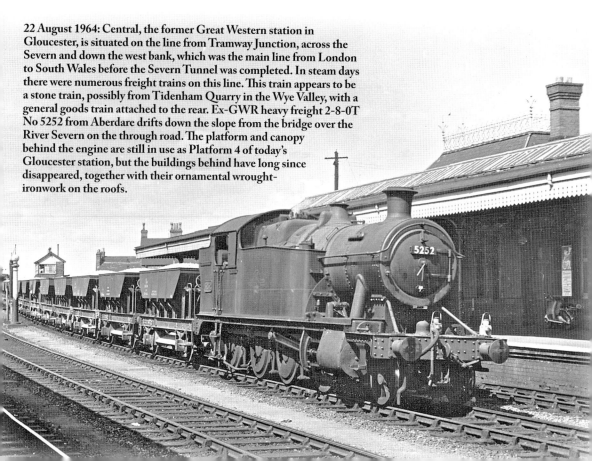

29 August 1964: BR Standard 4-6-0 No 73021 waits to leave the demolished side of Birmingham New Street for Gloucester.

Above 29 August 1964: No 73021 has just arrived at the south end of Gloucester (Eastgate) station with the train from Birmingham, while ex-LMS Class 5 No 44856 stands at the adjacent platform.

Below 29 August 1964: 'All points of the compass' – a 'Western' Class diesel-hydraulic enters the north end of the southbound platform at Gloucester (Eastgate) station. This location was very popular with local railway enthusiasts as all trains entering and leaving the north ends of both Eastgate and Central stations could be observed, and locomotives entering and leaving Horton Road shed, together with any standing in the nearest yard siding, could be recorded. The 'Western' is on train 1H60, the 4.55pm Paddington to Cheltenham 'Cheltenham Spa Express', and it is passing No 73021, which had earlier brought in my train from Birmingham (New Street). The Cheltenham train will reverse in the station and pass this point again in the opposite direction, probably hauled by a Gloucester-based tank engine to Cheltenham Spa (St James). In the background are a couple of ex-LMS 8F 2-8-0s in Horton Road shed yard.

Above **29 August 1964: That same evening 0-4-2T No 1472 leaves the northbound platform at Gloucester (Eastgate) towards the sidings. Horton Road shed can again be seen in the background, and the end of the southbound platform is occupied as usual by local trainspotters.**

Below **29 August 1964: Immediately after the previous photograph 'Castle' Class 4-6-0 No 7023 *Penrice Castle* departs towards Cheltenham with a train from the West of England. On the left is Gloucester Passenger Station signal box, a fine Midland Railway example, which controlled the movements from the station towards Tramway Junction, adjacent to Horton Road shed. Between the gas lamp post and the person a cast-iron Midland Railway trespass notice can be seen.**

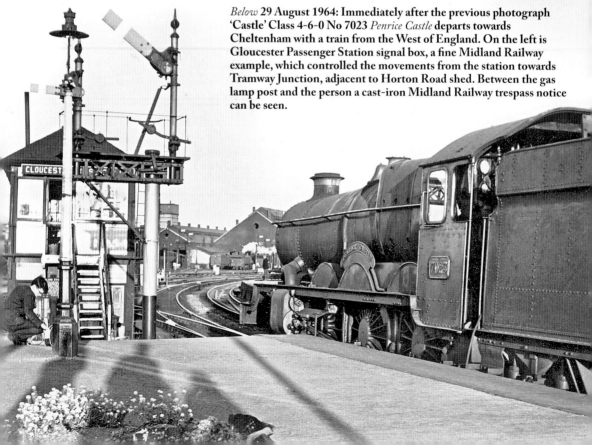

Above **29 August 1964:** The station buildings form the background for this second view of No 7023 *Penrice Castle*. The buildings are those of the second Gloucester (Eastgate) station, opened in 1896 and closed in 1975.

Below **29 August 1964:** After leaving Gloucester (Eastgate) station, trains for Bristol faced a climb up the incline to Tuffley Junction. After about a mile the line passed Tredworth Crossing, and the roof of the signal box is just visible above the second carriage of the train, photographed from the pavement of Stroud Road. The locomotive is ex-LMS Class 5 No 44919.

Above **29 August 1964: One of the problems with chalking reporting numbers on the smokeboxes of locomotives for specific trains was that, when they made the return journey, they were incorrect. This is case in this photograph of ex-GWR 'Castle' Class 4-6-0 No 5056** *Earl of Powis* **arriving at Cheltenham Spa (Malvern Road) station on a summer Saturday train taking me back to Birmingham (Snow Hill), which is still wearing the reporting number of its southbound journey.**

Right **29 August 1964: No 5056 is now seen at Stratford-upon-Avon. The loco shed is just visible immediately in front of the smokebox; this shed provided assisting locomotives to many trains such as this for the steep gradient out of Stratford to Earlswood.**

Above 5 September 1964: A week later I visited Gloucester (Central) station. At the extreme western end 2-6-2T No 416i waits with a local train for Hereford.

Below 5 September 1964: At the northern end of Gloucester (Central) station 0-4-2T No 1472 waits with a two-coach Chalford 'auto-train'. Just in front of the locomotive, across the platform, is the entrance to the long covered footbridge to Gloucester (Eastgate) station.

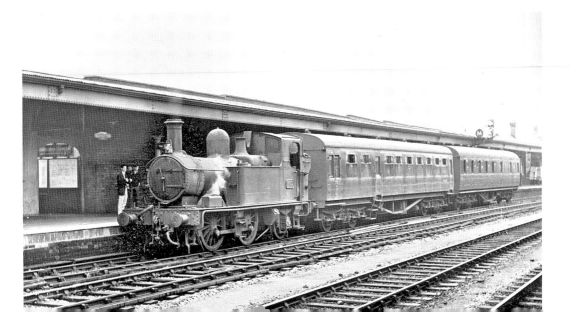

Left **5 September 1964: A typical Great Western fitted freight hauled by 2-8-0 No 3836 enters Gloucester (Central) station, passing Gloucester East signal box. In the background are locomotives in the Eastgate carriage sidings and the platforms at Eastgate station. Both signals in the foreground are fitted with 'calling on' arms below the main signal arms.**

Below **5 September 1964: BR(W) 'Modified Hall' Class 4-6-0 No 6994 *Baggrave Hall* calls at Stratford-upon-Avon with the summer Saturday 11.05am Ilfracombe to Wolverhampton train.**

Above **19 September 1964: An unusual broadside view of BR Standard 4-6-0 No 73093 standing at Platform 8 of Birmingham (New Street) station ready to take a train towards Worcester. During demolition and** rebuilding of the station, the wall and buildings between the old Queens Drive and Platform 7 were demolished, giving a clear view across to Platform 8 for a few days.

Right **October 1964:** On this October evening I was waiting at Cheltenham Spa (Lansdown) for a train to Gloucester when 'Castle' Class 4-6-0 No 7034 *Ince Castle* came in with a train for Gloucester. By this time steam locomotives on weekday trains were becoming very rare, and on the Worcester-Cheltenham-Gloucester line almost unheard of – fortunately I had my camera round my neck and took this photo with no preparation.

Top **October 1964: In 1964 steam locomotives were being scrapped at a tremendous rate, such that scrapyards could not take them fast enough, and large stocks of engines were stored awaiting scrapping. Here Sharpness Docks are being used for storing, and this scene shows about 17 locomotives, all Great Western types, awaiting the cutter's torch.**

Above **October 1964: Two 'County' Class 4-6-0s, cab-to-cab, await scrapping at Sharpness Docks. According to the chalked numbers they are Nos 1006** *County of Cornwall* **and 1027** *County of Stafford*.

Below **October 1964: Five of the locomotives awaiting scrapping at Sharpness Docks – that nearest the camera is one of the nine locomotives in the '4700' Class 2-8-0s, which were rarely photographed in action as their main duties were high-speed night freight trains. The second locomotive appears to be ex-GWR 'Castle' 4-6-0 No 7027** *Thornbury Castle*, **which was later moved to Barry; however, it avoided being cut up and is currently awaiting restoration.**

Above **October 1964: Sharpness was the terminus of branch trains from Berkeley Road or Gloucester from the time the Severn Bridge was knocked down until the service was withdrawn completely on 2 November 1964. One coach was normally sufficient for the skeleton service of four trains from Sharpness and three trains to Sharpness that operated in 1964. This view shows 0-6-0PT No 6412 waiting hopefully for some passengers with the last train of the day, the 6.00pm to Berkeley Road. Although the coach is an 'auto-coach' fitted for push-pull working, this was not used and the loco ran round at the end of each journey. Above the station roof can be seen the Severn Bridge Hotel.**

Below **October 1964: The loading gantry for the nuclear flasks used to transport nuclear waste from Berkeley Power Station can be seen in this view as No 6412 leaves with the 6.00pm train to Berkeley Road.**

Left **25 October 1964: A week before the Chalford 'auto-train' service was discontinued, ex-GWR 0-4-2T No 1458 leaves Ebley Crossing Halt with the push-pull train from Chalford to Gloucester. Steam issuing from every location, it propels the two coaches towards the next stop at Stonehouse (Burdett Road), which is now the only station open between Gloucester and Stroud.**

Below **25 October 1964: Sister locomotive No 1453, with its home-made smokebox number plate, calls at Ebley Crossing Halt with a train up the valley to Chalford.**

Left The official notice displayed inside the Chalford 'auto-trains' from August 1964. The withdrawal of services finally took place with affect from 2 November.

Below 25 October 1964: St Mary's Crossing Halt is the location for this view of the Chalford 'Auto' with the driver in his driving cab. Adjacent to the up line can be seen the three-car diesel stopping sign, which was rather optimistic in this rural location and unnecessary a week later when the halt closed. Once again the locomotive is No 1453.

British Railways Board
Transport Act 1962

Western Region

Withdrawal of railway passenger services

The Minister of Transport has given his consent to the Board's proposal to discontinue all passenger train services from the following stations and halts on the SWINDON—GLOUCESTER (Central) section of line:-

PURTON
MINETY & ASHTON KEYNES
OAKSEY HALT
CHALFORD
ST. MARY'S CROSSING HALT
BRIMSCOMBE

BRIMSCOMBE BRIDGE HALT
HAM MILL HALT
BOWBRIDGE CROSSING HALT
DOWNFIELD CROSSING HALT
CASHES GREEN HALT
EBLEY CROSSING HALT

The terms of the Minister's consent can be inspected at local booking offices

The date the services will be withdrawn will be announced later.

Left **25 October 1964: 0-4-2T No 1453 is seen again taking water from the platform water column at Stroud station, which has hardly altered since this photograph was taken.**

Below **25 October 1964:** Back at Ebley Crossing Halt, 0-4-2T No 1453 has discharged its passengers and waits to leave for Stonehouse (Burdett Rd) and Gloucester (Central). The type of passenger seriously affected by withdrawal of the service a week later is clearly in evidence – young mothers with children in prams are not so easily accommodated on the alternative bus services.

Main picture **2 November 1964:** This was also the last day of the Gloucester to Hereford train service, and 2-6-0 No 7318 is seen entering Blaisdon Halt with the 2.30pm Gloucester to Hereford train. After this day the little paraffin lantern hanging from the post on the right would not be required.

1965

Left **26 January 1965:** Designed by the Great Western Railway but built by British Railways, 'Castle' Class 4-6-0 No 7029 *Clun Castle* enters Gloucester (Eastgate) with an SLS special circular tour that had included the Devizes line earlier in the day. The train was routed back to Birmingham (Snow Hill) via Cheltenham and Stratford-upon-Avon. In the background is the Gloucester Leisure Centre under construction; the site of this photograph is now part of a supermarket car park.

Below **January 1965:** By contrast, this is 'Castle' Class No 7022 *Hereford Castle* (after its official withdrawal from service) employed on a permanent way relaying train at Brimscombe, in a very poor-looking state. The loco crew informed me that there was 'nothing wrong with her that an oily rag won't put right'!

Below **Early April 1965: Badgeworth was situated between Gloucester and Cheltenham on a stretch of track that was widened in 1942 to four tracks, but today is now down to two tracks again. This view shows an unidentified BR Class 4MT 4-6-0 of the '75xxx' series on a fully-fitted freight heading towards Cheltenham past Badgeworth signal box, which was constructed to a wartime austerity design when the line was widened.**

Below **Early April 1965: An ex-LMS 8F 2-8-0 follows on with a northbound freight.**

Above **Early April 1965: Looking north towards Cheltenham at Badgeworth we see a southbound freight hauled by heavy 'Prairie' 2-6-2T No 6128. This photograph and the previous two were all taken during a lunch break on a working day, showing how much freight still moved by rail in 1965.**

Left **24 April 1965: GWR 0-6-0PT No 6435 stands at Stratford-upon-Avon's former GWR station on the Birmingham (Snow Hill) to Cheltenham line with a Stephenson Locomotive Society special train to say 'Farewell to the Stratford-upon-Avon & Midland Junction Railway'. This engine was detached here and ex-LMS 0-6-0 No 44188, which had piloted No 6435 from Snow Hill, took the train onto the S&MJR.**

Above **5 May 1965:** BR Standard Class 9F 2-10-0 No 92215 hauls a freight past Tuffley Junction, where the former GWR line from Cheltenham to South Wales came alongside the LMS line from Gloucester (Eastgate) station. The junction in the name was that between the LMS main line and the branch line from the docks and the gasworks – there was no physical connection between the GWR and LMS lines.

Right **12 May 1965:** By this date all trains on the Oxford to Worcester line were diesel-hauled, but during a visit to Kingham a permanent way train arrived behind tender-first 'Manor' 4-6-0 No 7804 *Baydon Manor*. In the background can be seen the embankment that had carried the direct line from the Cheltenham branch (seen curving away to the left) to the Chipping Norton and Banbury branch, which turned away to the right. Note the unusual signal on the down platform, which is indicating that No 7804 has the track set for the Cheltenham direction, the other arm being for the main Worcester line.

Below **29 May 1965:** The Railway Correspondence & Travel Society ran its 'East Midlander' special using LNER 4-6-2 No 4472 *Flying Scotsman* through Gloucester using the former GWR route and the avoiding line from Gloucester South to Engine Shed Junction. The train stopped on the avoiding line for water and for the coal to be pulled forward in preparation for its journey northwards.

Bottom **29 May 1965:** 'The East Midlander' accelerates away from its water stop on the Gloucester avoiding line. A blind eye was turned to trespassing in order to view *Flying Scotsman*. Note the fair-haired boy nearest the locomotive – he is Peter Watts, now a railway book publisher!

Right **Summer 1965: Between Tuffley Junction and Standish Junction, south of Gloucester, the former LMS and GWR lines once ran side by side as four tracks. Very run-down 'Manor' 4-6-0 No 7829** *Ramsbury Manor*, **with all its name and number plates removed, is hauling a freight out of Gloucester in June or July 1965. The public right of way across the line here was the nearest point to my home for train watching, and the next few photographs were all taken from the footpath.**

Below **Summer 1965: An unidentified ex-LMS Class 5 approaches Gloucester on the former GWR line with a summer Saturday train, also in June or July of that year.**

Above **Summer 1965: Ex-LMS Class 5 No 45264 hauls a special freight of large concrete pipes along the former GWR up line just north of Standish Junction.**

Left **June 1965: The first station after Cheltenham Road (Malvern Road) on the line to Stratford-upon-Avon was Cheltenham Racecourse, which by this date was only used for special trains on race days and was becoming overgrown, as shown by the height of the weeds on the platforms. However, iron ore trains still passed through several times a day, and here we see a train of empty iron ore trucks hauled by BR 9F 2-10-0 No 92224 returning from South Wales to the East Midlands.**

Above **June 1965:** BR 5MT 4-6-0 No 73034 has charge of another train of empty iron ore trucks just north of Cheltenham Racecourse station, which is situated in the cutting in the distance. The line closed in 1976 but the Gloucestershire Warwickshire Railway has since reopened it as a successful heritage railway.

Below **July 1965:** We are now back at Badgeworth as an unidentified 'Grange' Class 4-6-0 hauls a partially fitted freight towards Cheltenham.

Above **31 July 1965: On summer Saturdays BR 'Britannia' 'Pacifics' were often pressed into service to operate the holiday trains to the West Country from the Midlands and the North. This rather dirty example is No 70053, formerly named** *Moray Firth***; it is heading the 10.05 Kingswear to Wolverhampton train at Haresfield Crossing between Standish Junction and Tuffley Junction.**

Above **31 July 1965:** 'Hall' Class 4-6-0 No 6916 *Misterton Hall*, with all its name and number plates removed, hauls a mixed freight on the former Great Western up line just north of Standish Junction, where a footpath crosses the tracks. The 'up' lines on this stretch are in opposite directions: the nearest track is the ex-LMS up line heading north towards Birmingham and Derby; the next track is the LMS down, towards Standish Junction and Bristol; the third track is the GWR down towards Gloucester, Cheltenham and Birmingham via Stratford-upon-Avon; and the track occupied by the train is the GWR up towards Standish Junction and Swindon, and with running powers over the LMS from Standish Junction to Yate.

Main picture **31 July 1965:** Another 'Britannia' 4-6-2, No 70045, formerly named *Lord Rowallan*, heads a summer Saturday train for the Midlands just north of Standish Junction. It is using the former GWR tracks and will pass Gloucester on the avoiding line.

Left **31 July 1965: Ex-GWR 'Grange' Class 4-6-0 No 6856** *Stowe Grange*, **with only its nameplates removed, passes light engine along the GWR up line just north of Standish Junction.**

Centre **31 July 1965: Ex-LMS Class 5 4-6-0 No 44983 leaves Cheltenham Spa (Lansdown) station for Gloucester. At this time the platforms ended just out of sight to the right of the picture, but since closure of the former GWR line to Stratford-upon-Avon (in the foreground) in July 1976 they have been extended right across this view.**

Below **31 July 1965: Ex-GWR 'Grange' Class 4-6-0 No 6855** *Saighton Grange* **stands at Cheltenham Spa (Malvern Road) with the 12.30 Penzance to Wolverhampton train. Behind the locomotive is the site of the engine shed, which was a sub-shed to Gloucester (Horton Road). Once again the engine is devoid of name and number plates.**

Left **31 July 1965:** The grimy No 6855 has now reached Stratford-upon-Avon with the Wolverhampton train. Despite its appearance, this locomotive took the train to Birmingham (Snow Hill) unassisted up the 1 in 75 incline between Stratford and Wilmcote. By this time the Midland Region had become responsible for the line and had installed an upper-quadrant starter signal. In the background a locomotive can be seen in Stratford-upon-Avon shed yard.

Centre **8 August 1965:** Lydbrook Viaduct carried the Severn & Wye (Midland & Great Western) Joint Railway across the Lydbrook valley between Mierystock and Lydbrook Junction, on the Ross-on-Wye to Monmouth Line. The line officially closed in January 1956, although the last train had run on 31 December 1952. The first photograph was taken in February 1962, when the only traffic across it were sheep, which occasionally fell off it into the gardens of houses below!

Below The second view shows demolition in progress in August 1965. The only traces now visible are some stonework where the stone arches met the embankments.

Above & below **9 August 1965: 'Manor' Class 4-6-0 No 7808** *Cookham Manor* **at The Reddings on the outskirts of Cheltenham with a train of steel products. Note the immaculate nature of the cutting sides – no trouble with leaves on the line is those days. No 7808 is now preserved at the Great Western Society's premises at Didcot.**

Above & below **9 August 1965:** The track maintenance gang stand back while BR 9F 2-10-0 No 92237 passes under The Reddings bridge with a northbound fully fitted train of vans. This gang must have been responsible for the immaculate nature of the track shown in the photographs taken in this area. It is not possible to deduce from the photograph which route the train will take northwards from Lansdown Junction, Cheltenham, as there was access to either the former LMS route through Ashchurch or the former GWR route through Stratford-upon-Avon.

10 August 1965: Between the sites of Hatherley Junction and Lansdown Junction there is a footbridge that was a popular train watching place and is still visited by enthusiasts to this day; the next three pictures were taken from it. In the first *(above)*, BR Standard 5MT 4-6-0 No 73070 is waiting for the track through Cheltenham Lansdown station to be vacated by the express that is overtaking it, hauled by D37. After the passage of the diesel-hauled train *(left)*, 73070 starts its train as a Brush Type 4 passes light engine towards Hatherley Junction, where the signal box was still standing although the branch line to Andoversford and Kingham had been built over by this date. The loco's tender is full of beautiful-looking coal – no wonder the safety valve is blowing off as the train moves slowly away.

10 August 1965: The next freight to pass under the footbridge near Hatherley Junction is a steel products train hauled by BR 9F 2-10-0 No 92150.

SLS Restored Engines Tour, 19 September 1965			
Station	Arrive	Depart	Loco(s)
Birmingham (Snow Hill)		10.30	4555, 1420
Stourbridge Junction	10.55	11.10	
Worcester (Shrub Hill)	11.53	12.30	
Bewdley	13.05	13.20	
Alveley Colliery Sidings	13.45	14.20	
Bewdley	14.50	15.00	
Dudley	(15.34)		
Wolverhampton (Low Level)	15.46	16.10	
Dudley	(16.22)		
Kidderminster	(16.48)		
Worcester (Shrub Hill)	17.10	17.40	3442
Stourbridge Junction	18.17	18.19	
Birmingham (Snow Hill)	18.43		
Only lineside photographs were obtained; the special was not travelled on.			

Above **19 September 1965: On another visit to Hatherley footbridge a close-up photograph of ex-LMS 8F 2-8-0 No 48517 was possible as it travelled towards Gloucester. Behind the tender can be seen the signal gantry for Lansdown Junction, showing the two possibilities of routing from there when travelling on either northbound line.**

Above **19 September 1965:** The Stephenson Locomotive Society (Midland Area) ran its 'Restored Engines Tour' on this Sunday. The train, hauled by GWR 2-6-2T No 4555 and GWR 0-4-2T No 1420, crosses the Victoria Bridge over the River Severn and head for Arley on the branch that is now the Severn Valley Railway.

Below **19 September 1965:** The SLS 'Restored Engines Tour' is now approaching Churchill & Blakedown station between Kidderminster and Stourbridge. The train then went on to Wolverhampton (Low Level) via Dudley.

Above & below **19 September 1965: The tour is seen again near Churchill & Blakedown returning from Wolverhampton (Low level) to Worcester (Shrub Hill) in the late afternoon.**

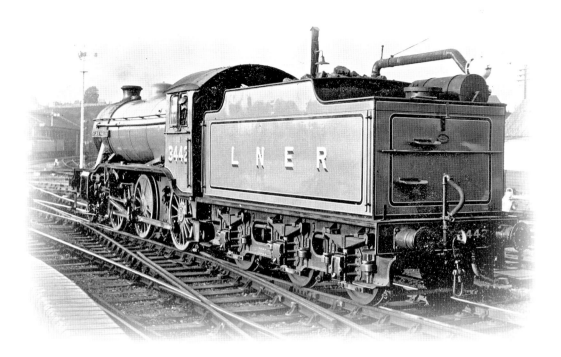

Above **19 September 1965:** The SLS special reversed at Worcester (Shrub Hill) and returned to Birmingham (Snow Hill) via Stourbridge Junction behind LNER 2-6-0 No 3442 *The Great Marquess*. The locomotive is seen here running forward from the centre line at Worcester ready to reverse over the trackwork in the foreground and join the train. Worcester shed is in the background, with a Brush Type 4 diesel standing outside.

Below **19 September 1965:** *The Great Marquess* waits to depart from Worcester at 17.40 for Birmingham (Snow Hill) via Stourbridge Junction. At this time the locomotive was owned by Viscount Garnock and carried a Canadian bell, which he had brought back from Canada.

19 September 1965: The SLS 'Restored Engines Tour' leaves Worcester (Shrub Hill) station for Birmingham (Snow Hill).

Above 19 September 1965: After the rail tour had left Worcester Nos 4555 and 1420 reversed out of the platform onto Worcester shed.

Below 19 September 1965: Meanwhile the special headed towards Birmingham, and is seen here just north of Worcester behind No 3442.

SLS 'Final GWR Cavalcade', 17 October 1965			
Station	**Arrive**	**Depart**	**Loco(s)**
Birmingham (Snow Hill)		10.15	6667
Stourbridge Junction	10.41	10.44	
Worcester (Shrub Hill)	11.20	11.30	6435, 1420
Ashchurch	12.04	12.14	
Gloucester South	13.02	13.12	6435, 7029
Bristol (Temple Meads)	15.00	16.00	7029
Gloucester (Eastgate)	16.48	16.57	
Worcester (Shrub Hill)	17.35	17.43	
Stourbridge Junction	18.18	18.23	
Birmingham (Snow Hill)	18.50		

Below **17 October 1965: Worcester (Shrub Hill) was foggy at 11.20 on this Sunday morning when 0-6-2T No 6667 arrived with the Stephenson Locomotive Society's 'Final GWR Cavalcade' tour from Birmingham (Snow Hill) to Bristol (Temple Meads) and return. This locomotive left the train at Worcester to be replaced by 0-6-0PT No 6435 and 0-4-2T No 1420.**

Above **17 October 1965: Nos 1420 and 6435 move forward off the centre track ready to reverse onto the train.**

Below **17 October 1965: Ashchurch station was a photographic stop for the SLS special. It was still a little foggy but the usual line of photographers took their pictures of this unusual double-header.**

Above **17 October 1965: The 'Final GWR Cavalcade' rail tour had a locomotive change on the Gloucester avoiding line; Nos 1420 and 6435 were uncoupled and 'Castle' Class 4-6-0 No 7029** *Clun Castle* **backed onto the train. It then became a very unusual double-leader when 0-6-0PT No 6435 piloted the 'Castle' to Bristol.**

Below **17 October 1965: Bristol (Temple Meads) can rarely have witnessed a more unusual arrival as Nos 6435 and 7029 entered the station from Gloucester.**

Above **17 October 1965: No 6435 has surrendered the SLS special headboard to** *Clun Castle* **at Bristol (Temple Meads) in preparation for the 'Castle' to return the 'Final GWR Cavalcade' special to Birmingham (Snow Hill). An array of diesel locomotives occupies Bristol Bath Road shed yard as the pannier tank moves off.**

Below **17 October 1965: No 7029** *Clun Castle* **takes water at Gloucester (Eastgate) while returning the extraordinary SLS special to Birmingham (Snow Hill) via Stourbridge Junction.**

Left **20 November 1965:**
Preserved Great Western 'Castle'
Class 4-6-0 No 4079 *Pendennis*
Castle **stops at Gloucester**
(Eastgate) on a Locomotive
Club of Great Britain special.
This locomotive was sold to the
Hammersley Iron Company in
Dampier, Australia, in 1977 and
resided there until its recent
repatriation.

Below **20 November 1965: In**
very poor light the LCGB
special makes a rousing exit from
Gloucester. In the distance behind
the signal is the unique Barton
Street Junction signal box perched
high above the tracks on girders.
The line in the foreground lead to
the Sudbrook Yard branch down to
Gloucester Docks.

1966

1966

'Pannier Tank Farewell Tour', 11 September 1966

Station	Arrive	Depart	Loco(s)
Birmingham (Snow Hill)		10.30	9610, 9630
Dudley (via Swan Village)			
Halesowen	10.57	11.20	
Old Hill	11.30	11.55	
Dudley	12.10	12.45	
Wolverhampton (Low Level)	13.00	14.20	
Birmingham (Snow Hill)	(14.40)		
Henley-in-Arden	(15.04)		
Stratford-upon-Avon	15.17	16.05	
Leamington Spa	16.30	17.15	
Hatton	(17.26)		
Birmingham (Snow Hill)	17.50		

Right 11 September 1966: The Stephenson Locomotive Society (Midland Area) organised a special train to bid farewell to the pannier tanks. The only two panniers in a fit state to undertake the tour were Nos 9630 and 9610 of Wrexham (Croes Newydd), which were duly borrowed for the day. Having visited Dudley, the panniers needed to replenish their water supplies and this is being undertaken at Old Hill on the remnant of the Halesowen branch. The pipe from the tank and the hose leaked a little!

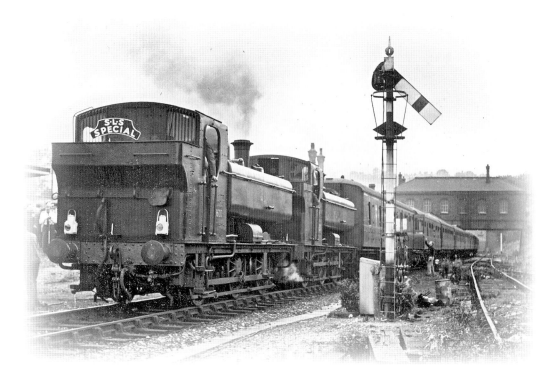

Above **11 September 1966: The 'Pannier Tank Farewell Tour' stands at Dudley station. The two panniers have lost their cabside number plates.**

Below **11 September 1966: Three Palethorpes sausage vans are parked out of use at Dudley. These vans were attached to express trains to all parts of the Western Region from the Palethorpes sausage factory at Calne in Wiltshire, but by that time the traffic had been transferred to road haulage.**

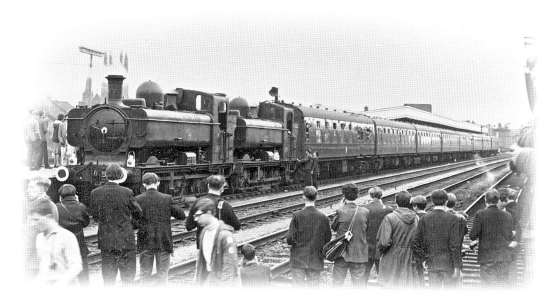

Above 11 September 1966: Leamington Spa was a reversing point towards the end of the tour. The train arrived in the up platform from Stratford-upon-Avon, with the locomotives running bunker-first at the other end of the train. This photograph was taken as the locomotives coupled up to the coaches in preparation for the run back to Birmingham (Snow Hill). Photographers were allowed to stand on the down main.

Below 11 September 1966: After coupling onto the coaches 0-6-0PT Nos 9610 and 9630 propelled the coaches out of the station and returned to the down platform in preparation for the return to Birmingham. After leaving Leamington the two panniers and their eight coaches reached a speed in excess of 60mph up Hatton Bank in a hair-raising dash for Birmingham. Unfortunately No 9630 blew the front end out of one of its cylinders between Hatton and Lapworth and had to be shunted off the train by No 9610 and dumped at Lapworth. The latter completed the tour on its own, but afterwards retired to Tyseley shed with four hot axleboxes. Farewell to the panniers!

Index of locations